Art of War

Also from EATMS Productions

Books on power, survival, women's autonomy, and the systems shaping modern America.

Nonfiction

Billionaires, Capitalism, and Power

Evil and the Mountain Ungreed
Self Help for American Billionaires
Selfish Steve and the Ivory Tower
Tariffs, Taxes, & Face-Eating Leopards
Ban Billionaires: Fascism Fix

Fascism, Religion, and Cultural Control

Self Help for the Manosphere
Fascism 2025
Fascism & the Perverts & the Greed Virus
Christian Fascism Marriage Book
Tyranny, Table Manners, & Tiramisu

Guides for Women's Autonomy and Protection

How to Survive in Post-America as a Woman
Project 2025 American Drag
4B – Burn, Ban, Boycott, Build
4B OG – So No Go GYN
I'm Glad He's Dead

Analysis of Authoritarian Project 2025

Project 2025: The Blueprint
Project 2025: The List
Project 2025, Christian Dumb Dumbs, & The Republican Agenda
Fascism, Project 2025, & The Pinkprint

Modern Rewrites for Women

Stoic Principles Reimagined
Siddhartha Reimagined
The Prince Reimagined for Women
The Art of War Reimagined for Women
The Jungle Reimagined
The Constitution Reimagined for Women

Machine Learning Series

AI, Bitcoin, Nostr for Women
AI, Safety, & Security for Women
AI, Anxiety, & Health for Women
AI, Kids, & Family Safety for Women
AI, Creativity, & Personal Expression for Women
AI, Independent Work, & Parallel Power for Women

Social Systems Series

Emotional Labor for Women
Household Power for Women
Workplace Power for Women
Medical Bias for Women
Aging Systems for Women
Recovery Systems for Women

Fiction

Dystopian Stories of Resistance and Collapse

Propaganda Paige & the Missing Prosperity
Propaganda Paige & the TIDE Manifesto
Propaganda Paige & the Shadow Cartographers
Propaganda Paige & the Prosperity Alliance
Propaganda Paige & the Shattered Truth
Propaganda Paige & the Rising TIDE
Propaganda Paige & the Last Bastion
Propaganda Paige & the Dawn of Prosperity
Project 2025: Dorian — The Last Men
Project 2025: Boy — A Last Men Novel

The Art of War Reimagined
For Women 2025

Sympathy & Support 3

by

Hanna Frasier

EATMS
PRODUCTIONS

ISBN: 978-1-966014-17-1

Cover, interior design, interior prints by: Esme Mees

eatms@pm.me
www.eatms.me

Printed in the United States of America.

When men are oppressed, it's a tragedy.
When women are oppressed, it's tradition.

— Letty Cotton Pogrebin

Table of Contents

Introduction—Women's Art of War in 2025   9

Chapter 1—Know Your Enemy, Know Yourself   17

Chapter 2—Mapping the Terrain of Oppression   27

Chapter 3—Strategic Patience and Timing   39

Chapter 4—Divide and Conquer the Patriarchy   51

Chapter 5—The Element of Surprise   65

Chapter 6— Winning Without Fighting   79

Chapter 7—Resilience in Battle   93

Chapter 8—Adopting to Change   107

Chapter 9—Defining Victory   121

Chapter 10—Securing the Future   133

Chapter 11—Leaving a Legacy   147

Conclusion—Women's Art of War – NOW   159

About EATMS Productions   168

Introduction
Women's Art of War in 2025

War is an ugly word, one that men have wrapped in glory and mythology, draped in flags, and carved into marble monuments. War is the conquest of land, the domination of bodies, the endless cycle of destruction and reconstruction that fuels power and greed. But war is also a concept far older than weapons, older than history itself, it is strategy, survival, the art of knowing when to strike, when to retreat, and when to reshape the battlefield entirely. And if there is one truth women have always known, it is that we have been at war since the beginning. Not the kind of war that is sung about in ballads or written into history books, no, the wars women fight are insidious, unrecognized, woven into the fabric of daily life. It is the war of being spoken over, of being paid less, of carrying the burden of unpaid labor, of watching decisions about our bodies made by those who do not inhabit them. It is the war of expectation, where the demand to be small, silent, and accommodating never ceases, and the moment a woman dares to step beyond her assigned place, she is met with resistance as fierce as any standing army.

Sun Tzu's *The Art of War* has been dissected, repackaged, and applied to everything from business to football to personal success, but always from the vantage point of those already in power. His lessons, on deception, on patience, on knowing both oneself and one's enemy, have been co-opted by generals, CEOs, and strategists who see the world as a game to be won. But what happens when those same lessons are placed in the hands of women, the very people who have been treated as pawns rather than players? What does it mean to reimagine war, not as an act of destruction, but as a form of radical strategy for survival, autonomy, and ultimately, transformation? The women of today do not need another empowerment speech about leaning in, about breaking glass ceilings that will only be rebuilt the moment we leave the room. We need a playbook, a strategy guide that does not ask for permission or beg for change but instead operates with the clear-eyed recognition that the game itself is rigged, and that the only way forward is to outthink, outmaneuver, and reshape the battlefield entirely.

This is not a call to arms in the traditional sense. It is a call to strategy. Women have always been forced to fight battles, but rarely have we been given the space to define the terms of engagement. This book is about reclaiming that power, not through brute force, but through understanding, precision, and disruption. It is about seeing the structures of oppression not as immovable forces but as flawed systems with cracks and vulnerabilities that can be exploited. It is about recognizing that the terrain of battle has shifted; that war is no longer fought on distant battlefields but in courtrooms, workplaces, legislative halls, and digital spaces where narratives are shaped and futures are decided. It is about harnessing the quiet, often underestimated power that has always been at women's disposal, the ability to observe, to plan, to build alliances in the shadows, to strike when the moment is right, and to reshape the very rules of the game.

For too long, women have been told that our greatest strength is in our ability to nurture, to compromise, to be the reasonable counterbalance to men's aggression. But what if strength means something else entirely? What if true strength is knowing when to walk away and when to stand your ground? What if power is not just about gaining a seat at the table but about dismantling the table altogether? What if winning is not about playing by their rules but rewriting them? This book does not offer easy answers. What it offers is a way

10

of thinking, a way of seeing the world through a strategic lens that has long been denied to women. It is about understanding that every choice we make, whether in politics, business, relationships, or daily life, is a move in a larger game, and those who refuse to play are still, inevitably, being played.

Women have always been warriors, though history has tried to erase or soften our battles. This is not a new war, but it is one that must be fought with new tactics. The strategies laid out in these pages are not about aggression for aggression's sake. They are about reclaiming control, about choosing the battles that matter, about knowing when to retreat in order to win the war. They are about understanding power, not just how it operates against us, but how we can wield it in return. Because make no mistake: this is war. But this time, we are not asking for permission to fight.

The myth of fairness is one of the greatest weapons patriarchy has ever wielded. It tells women that if we work hard enough, prove ourselves enough, and play by the rules, we will be rewarded. It dangles equality like a prize at the end of an impossible race, whispering that if we are patient, if we do not complain too loudly, if we do not demand too much, then justice will find its way to us. But fairness has never been the foundation of this world, and the idea that systems built by men for the benefit of men will one day, out of sheer moral awakening, decide to uplift women is a dangerous lie. The truth is that power is rarely given; it is taken, seized by those who understand that waiting is a losing game.

The history of women's rights is not a story of benevolent men waking up one day and deciding to be kind. It is a history of relentless pressure, of strategic disruption, of forcing hands that refused to move. Women did not get the right to vote by politely asking. Women did not gain reproductive rights through patience. Women did not enter the workforce, demand equal pay, or push against the walls of oppression because they believed in fairness, they did it because they recognized that the game was rigged, and they learned how to beat it.

What Sun Tzu understood, and what men in power have used to their advantage for centuries, is that victory is not always about strength. It is about knowledge, patience, manipulation, and the ability to see the battlefield clearly when others are blinded by arrogance or emotion. Women have been conditioned to believe that strategy is a masculine trait, that aggression is unbecoming, that ambition must be softened with humility.

But what if we reject that conditioning? What if we recognize that every day we are already employing the very tactics Sun Tzu describes, reading rooms, anticipating reactions, navigating danger, adapting to shifting power dynamics, just to exist in a world that was never designed for us? The difference is that we have not been taught to name these skills as strategy, and we have not been encouraged to wield them deliberately. Instead, we have been told to shrink ourselves, to apologize for our ambition, to be grateful for scraps of power rather than seizing what we deserve. That ends now.

Women's wars have always been fought in the shadows, in whispers, in unspoken negotiations and quiet acts of defiance. We have survived by reading the intentions of men before they even speak, by predicting danger before it arrives, by moving through a world that underestimates us at every turn. But survival is not enough. If the past few years have shown us anything, it is that no amount of progress is guaranteed, that rights once thought secured can be clawed back the moment those in power decide they have tolerated women's freedom for long enough. We cannot afford to keep playing defense. We cannot afford to sit back and hope that the next election, the next policy shift, the next wave of cultural change will finally be the one to deliver us from oppression. The only way forward is with strategy, with precision, with an understanding that power is not a thing to be requested, it is a thing to be taken.

The battlefield is everywhere. It is in our workplaces, where women are still paid less than men for the same labor. It is in our homes, where unpaid domestic work and emotional labor remain expectations rather than choices. It is in our bodies, where laws are written not to protect us but to control us. It is in politics, where women are still outnumbered, still dismissed, still expected to fight twice as hard for half the recognition. It is in media, where our stories are twisted to fit narratives that serve the powerful, where our anger is portrayed as hysteria, where our ambition is called ruthless while men's is simply expected. The war is not coming, it is here, and it always has been. The only question that remains is whether we will finally start fighting it on our own terms.

This book is not about teaching women to be angry. Anger is easy, and anger without strategy is a trap that those in power use to discredit, to exhaust, to divide. This book is about teaching women to think like generals, to see every interaction, every challenge, every obstacle as a battlefield where victory is determined not by brute force but by clarity, calculation, and the refusal to play by rules designed to keep us losing. It is about knowing when to be patient and when to strike. It is about building alliances, identifying weaknesses in the structures that oppress us, and exploiting them with precision. It is about reshaping the fight so that we are not reacting to attacks but dictating the terms of engagement. Because if history has proven anything, it is that those who control the battlefield control the future. And women have spent far too long letting others decide the shape of our future for us. That ends now.

There is a reason history books have always been written by men. Those who control the narrative control the way the world understands power, legitimacy, and justice. For centuries, the stories of war, leadership, and strategy have been framed as masculine endeavors, as though cunning, resilience, and intelligence are traits that only men possess. Women's contributions have been erased, downplayed, or rewritten to fit the mold of passive support rather than active leadership. When women have led revolutions, when they have waged war, when they have seized power, the record has often been buried beneath layers of distortion. Joan of Arc was turned into a saint rather than a strategist. Cleopatra was reduced to a seductress rather than a political mastermind. Women's victories have been treated as exceptions, as accidents of history, rather than the result of deliberate action and calculated strategy. This distortion is not accidental. It is part of a larger system designed to convince women that power is not ours to claim, that leadership is not our birthright, and that strategy is a game played by men while we sit quietly on the sidelines, waiting to be rescued or granted small privileges in exchange for our compliance.

The greatest trick patriarchy ever pulled was convincing women that we are not warriors. That to fight back, to take power, to challenge authority is unnatural, unfeminine, unbecoming. That ambition in men is leadership, but in women, it is arrogance. That power in men is destiny, but in women, it is dangerous. And yet, if women had not fought, we would still be living as property, our bodies and labor owned and controlled without question. If women had not strategized, if we had not built alliances, if we had not learned how to work within and around the systems designed to keep us silent, we would not have gained the right to vote, to work, to control our own finances, to refuse marriage, to access birth control.

Every single right we have today was won through struggle, through careful planning, through persistence, through sheer force of will. And yet, even as we stand on the shoulders of those who fought before us, we are told that our war is over. That we have enough. That we should be satisfied with what we have been given. That asking for more, demanding true equality, pushing beyond the boundaries they have set for us, is selfish, radical, unreasonable. But those boundaries are not real. They are an illusion, upheld only by our continued willingness to believe in them.

What this book offers is not another set of hollow empowerment slogans or feel-good affirmations. It is not about telling women to be confident while ignoring the systems that punish them for their confidence. It is not about pretending that we can manifest our way to equality if we just work hard enough, stay positive enough, or lean in far enough. This book is about reality. About the world as it is, not as we wish it to be. It is about understanding power as it operates, not as it pretends to operate. It is about seeing the battlefield clearly and using every tool at our disposal to navigate it with intelligence, precision, and purpose. This book is about winning, not in the way men have defined it, through brute force and domination, but in the way women have always understood it: through adaptability, through collective strength, through playing a long game that outlasts and outmaneuvers the forces that seek to keep us small.

The women who will read this book are not waiting to be told that they are strong. They already know it. They live it every day in the choices they make, the obstacles they overcome, the fights they are already engaged in, whether in politics, in business, in activism, or simply in the struggle to exist in a world that was not built with them in mind. What they need is a strategy. A new way of thinking about power, control, and action. A framework for engaging with the forces that shape their lives, not from a place of reaction but from a place of deliberate, calculated intent. What they need is not another pep talk about how things will get better if we just stay hopeful, it is a manual for how to make things better, how to shift the balance of power, how to move through the world with the kind of strategic awareness that ensures we are not merely surviving, but winning.

The strategies laid out in these pages are drawn from the wisdom of Sun Tzu, but they are not his alone. They are the strategies women have always used, whether they were recognized for it or not. They are the tactics of revolutionaries, of leaders, of mothers, of workers, of survivors. They are the quiet, relentless maneuvers that have chipped away at patriarchy piece by piece, that have turned small victories into lasting change. And now, they are named, written, and offered as tools for the battles ahead. Because the war is not over, and the time for hoping that fairness will one day find us has passed. This is not about waiting. This is about taking. This is about winning on our terms. And it starts now.

1
Know Your Enemy, Know Yourself

The first and most fundamental rule of strategy is knowing who and what you are up against. Sun Tzu understood that battles are not won through brute strength alone but through intelligence, foresight, and a deep understanding of both the enemy and oneself. Yet, for women, this wisdom has long been buried beneath the expectation that we should not name our enemies, that we should not acknowledge the forces working against us, that we should instead be grateful for the progress already made.

The world tells us to be patient, to negotiate, to assume good faith even in the face of overwhelming evidence to the contrary. We are taught to second-guess our own instincts, to soften our anger, to explain away the systemic injustices we experience as misunderstandings or unfortunate realities rather than deliberate mechanisms of control. But ignorance is not an advantage, and refusing to see the battlefield for what it truly is does not keep us safe, it only makes us easier to defeat.

To know the enemy is to strip away the illusions that keep us complacent. The enemy is not just an individual man in a boardroom talking over you, nor is it only the politician drafting laws to strip away your bodily autonomy. The enemy is the system itself, the interlocking structures of power that protect and perpetuate male dominance across politics, economics, culture, and even personal relationships. It is the social conditioning that teaches boys entitlement and girls compliance, the economic policies that ensure women remain

underpaid and overworked, the judicial system that punishes
women more harshly for defending themselves than it does
men for perpetrating violence. It is the deeply embedded bias
in media that portrays ambitious men as visionaries and
ambitious women as unlikable, that punishes women for aging
while rewarding men for the same, that frames male violence
as an individual failing but female resistance as hysteria. It is
the myth of meritocracy that tells women to work harder while
rigging the game in favor of those who never had to prove
their worth in the first place.

But knowing the enemy is not enough. The second half of the
equation is knowing yourself, and this is where women have
been deliberately sabotaged from the beginning. For centuries,
we have been conditioned to distrust our own instincts, to seek
external validation, to measure our worth through the eyes of
men and the standards of a society that was never designed to
serve us. We have been taught that power is unseemly, that
ambition is dangerous, that confidence must always be
tempered with humility. Women who assert themselves too
much are labeled difficult, aggressive, unlikeable. Women who
demand fairness are called ungrateful. Women who refuse to
smile are told they are too cold, while those who try to be
approachable are dismissed as unserious. This is not
accidental. It is a tactic of control, a way to keep women so
focused on shaping themselves into an acceptable form that
they never stop to question why the rules are different for them
in the first place.

To know yourself is to break free from this conditioning. It is
to recognize the power that has always been yours, even if the
world has tried to convince you otherwise. It is to understand
your strengths, not just in the ways that have been deemed
socially acceptable, but in the ways that challenge the system
itself. Women are already masters of strategy in ways we rarely
acknowledge. We have learned, out of necessity, to navigate
dangerous situations with precision, to anticipate threats
before they materialize, to read between the lines of what is

said and unsaid in boardrooms, relationships, and social interactions. We have had to develop emotional intelligence not as a luxury but as a survival skill. These are not weaknesses. These are weapons. But they can only be wielded effectively when we recognize them for what they are.

This chapter is about dismantling the narratives that have kept women from embracing their full strategic potential. It is about shifting the way we see both our opposition and ourselves. To know your enemy is to stop making excuses for the forces that seek to control you. To know yourself is to stop waiting for permission to be powerful. The war against women has never been declared outright, but it has been waged for centuries. The only question left is whether we will finally start fighting it with our eyes open.

Recognizing the enemy is one thing; recognizing the enemy's tactics is another. Oppression does not sustain itself through brute force alone. It is maintained through misdirection, normalization, and the slow erosion of self-worth. The most effective systems of control do not simply tell people what to do, they convince them that there is no alternative. They do not simply block opportunities, they convince those on the margins that they were never meant to have those opportunities in the first place. Patriarchy does not survive because women are incapable of leadership, strength, or power, it survives because it has mastered the art of convincing women to doubt themselves, to question their own instincts, to waste energy seeking approval from the very forces that keep them in place. This is why knowing yourself is just as critical as knowing the enemy. Because the most effective form of oppression is one that convinces its target to participate in their own subjugation.

Women are taught from a young age to see power as something external, something to be earned through the approval of others rather than something innate. We are conditioned to believe that we must be chosen, validated, deemed worthy by institutions, by men, by the unwritten rules of social hierarchy. We are told to wait, to wait to be asked, to wait to be given a turn, to wait for the world to recognize our value. And when that recognition does not come, we are told to blame ourselves. Work harder, be more likable, adjust, accommodate, soften the edges of your ambition, make your success look effortless, never let them see you struggle. The rules shift constantly, the expectations remain contradictory, and the goalposts are always moving. This is not a design flaw in the system, it is the design. If women spend all their energy trying to mold themselves into something acceptable, they will have nothing left for rebellion.

To break free from this cycle, women must first understand that self-doubt is not an accident, it is an inheritance. It is the result of generations of deliberate conditioning designed to keep us from recognizing our own power. The messages are everywhere, woven into the fabric of our cultures, our institutions, our relationships. Women are given praise for being accommodating, for putting others before themselves, for making sacrifices. We are taught that our worth is in our ability to support, to nurture, to step aside. When we are assertive, we are told to tone it down. When we demand fairness, we are called difficult. When we succeed, we are met with suspicion, who helped her? Did she really earn it? There is no version of a successful woman that does not come with an asterisk, and that is by design.

But here is the truth that patriarchy does not want women to realize: there is no power more dangerous than a woman who knows exactly who she is. A woman who has stopped apologizing. A woman who has stopped seeking permission. A woman who is no longer waiting to be chosen. Because once a woman stops playing the game on the system's terms, the system loses its hold over her. Once she stops seeing self-doubt as an innate flaw and recognizes it as an implanted strategy of control, she can begin the work of unlearning it. She can begin to see herself not as someone who must constantly prove her worth, but as someone who has had that worth all along. This chapter is not about empty empowerment slogans or surface-level confidence tricks. It is about something deeper, something more dangerous. It is about taking back the tools that have been used against us and wielding them in our favor. It is about strategy, not sentiment.

To know yourself is to see the mechanisms of control for what they are. To know your enemy is to understand that their greatest weapon has never been force, it has been the slow, steady dismantling of your belief in yourself. Reversing that damage is not easy. It requires deliberate effort, constant vigilance, and a willingness to question everything we have been taught. But once that work begins, once the illusions start to break down, the real battle can finally begin. And this time, it will not be fought on their terms.

Once you see the mechanisms of control for what they are, you can never unsee them. The world will try to convince you that your realization is an overreaction, that you are imagining patterns where none exist, that the barriers you see are not real but rather products of your own shortcomings. That is how systemic oppression perpetuates itself, not by simply existing, but by making its targets doubt its existence. The most effective enemy is one that convinces you it does not exist at all. Women who begin to recognize these patterns are often met with backlash, not just from the obvious sources, men in power, institutions designed to maintain male dominance, but from those who have internalized the system so deeply that they mistake their own oppression for normalcy.

You will hear it from other women, the ones who have spent a lifetime playing by the rules and do not want to believe the game was rigged all along. You will hear it from people who claim to be allies but who urge you to be reasonable, to not push too hard, to not alienate those in power by being too direct, too forceful, too unwilling to compromise. You will hear it from within yourself, in the voice that patriarchy has implanted in all of us, the voice that asks, "What if they're right? What if I'm overreacting? What if this is just how things are?" That voice is not yours. It is an echo of centuries of conditioning, of a world that benefits from your hesitation. The moment you recognize it as such, its power begins to fade.

But awareness alone is not enough. Knowing that a system is rigged does not dismantle it. Understanding that you have been conditioned to doubt yourself does not immediately erase that conditioning. That is why strategy is essential. Sun Tzu did not simply teach warriors to recognize their enemies, he taught them to use that knowledge to anticipate attacks, to shape the battlefield, to make their enemy's strengths into weaknesses. The same principle applies here. Once you recognize that self-doubt has been deliberately cultivated in you, you can start to use that knowledge against the system that implanted it.

You stop second-guessing yourself every time you demand fairness. You stop apologizing for your ambition, your anger, your refusal to tolerate less than what you deserve. You begin to see that every hesitation, every instinct to soften your words, every time you consider making yourself smaller to avoid conflict, it is all part of a system designed to keep you contained. And once you stop cooperating with that system, once you refuse to internalize the guilt it tries to place on you, you become something truly dangerous: a woman who no longer plays by their rules.

Understanding your own power is not a process that happens overnight. It requires undoing years, sometimes decades, of training that has taught you to seek approval, to avoid confrontation, to tolerate injustice because fighting back is inconvenient, exhausting, or simply too risky. It requires questioning relationships that may have once seemed harmless but now reveal themselves as reinforcing your subjugation. It requires recalibrating your sense of self-worth, not by external validation but by an internal certainty that you do not need permission to take up space, to demand respect, to fight for your place in the world. And most of all, it requires patience. The world does not change overnight. Systems of power do not collapse because we wish them to. But strategy is about playing the long game, about recognizing that every action, every refusal to comply, every moment of defiance is another crack in the foundation of an outdated order. And cracks, given enough time, turn into collapses.

Knowing your enemy and knowing yourself are not two separate battles; they are the same. The clearer you see the system for what it is, the clearer you see yourself within it, not as a passive player but as an active force capable of reshaping the rules. This is why self-awareness is not just an exercise in personal growth but an act of rebellion. Because once you know yourself, once you truly, deeply, unshakably know yourself, the system loses its ability to define you. And when that happens, you stop being just another player in their game. You become the one rewriting the rules.

Once you have stripped away the illusions, once you have seen the enemy for what it is and reclaimed the parts of yourself that the system tried to break, the question becomes: what now? Awareness without action is stagnation. It is not enough to simply know the enemy or understand how the system operates if that knowledge does not translate into movement, into strategy, into power. Too often, women are encouraged to stop at awareness, to rest in the knowledge that they have correctly diagnosed the problem but are given no tools to address it. This is deliberate. The system is more than happy to let women discuss oppression so long as those discussions remain theoretical, so long as they do not disrupt the order of things.

Even within feminism, there has been a long history of centering analysis over action, of turning injustice into something to be studied rather than something to be dismantled. But knowing your enemy, knowing yourself, these are not academic exercises. They are steps toward something larger. They are meant to sharpen, to prepare, to position you for the next move.

That next move will not look the same for every woman. Strategy is not one-size-fits-all, and power does not come in a singular form. Some women will fight on the front lines of activism, disrupting systems through direct confrontation. Some will work from within institutions, using their positions to shift policies, to reshape power from the inside. Some will build alternatives entirely, refusing to operate within a structure that was never meant to serve them. And some will resist in quieter, but no less radical ways, by refusing to comply with expectations, by withdrawing their labor from systems that exploit them, by teaching the next generation not to accept the limitations placed upon them.

Every one of these actions is a battlefield, every one of these choices a strategic move. The mistake is in believing that there is only one way to fight, that power only looks like what men have defined it to be. The reality is that women have always wielded power, even in the moments when history refused to acknowledge it. The key is in recognizing it as such and using it with intention.

But strategy requires more than just action; it requires endurance. The fight against oppression is not a single battle, not a momentary rebellion that will resolve itself in one generation, one movement, one political victory. It is an ongoing war, and the forces that seek to suppress women's power are adaptable, relentless, and deeply entrenched. This is why self-knowledge must be more than just an intellectual exercise. It must be a foundation, a grounding force that allows women to sustain themselves even when the enemy shifts tactics, even when the battlefield changes, even when the costs feel unbearable.

Burnout is not just a personal issue; it is a tool of oppression. The system counts on exhaustion, on discouragement, on women becoming so drained by the fight that they retreat, that they resign themselves to the way things are. It relies on infighting, on division, on making women believe that their battles are separate rather than interconnected. Knowing yourself means recognizing these tactics, anticipating them, and refusing to let them break you.

The final truth of war, the one that every strategist must understand, is that victory is not always immediate. The best plans unfold over time, with patience, with adjustments, with an eye not just on the next move but on the endgame. Women have been trained to think in terms of survival, of making it through the next crisis, the next obstacle, the next exhausting battle against sexism, discrimination, and systemic violence. But the greatest threat to the system is not women who are simply surviving, it is women who are planning for something beyond survival.

Women who are building, strategizing, reshaping the world not just to accommodate their presence but to center their power. The enemy has counted on women staying reactive, staying scattered, staying unsure of their own abilities. The moment that changes, the moment women stop waiting for justice and start creating it, the war is no longer theirs to control.

Knowing your enemy is about stripping them of their ability to operate in secrecy, about calling out the mechanisms they use to maintain their grip on power. Knowing yourself is about refusing to internalize the limitations they have placed upon you, about reclaiming the strength, intelligence, and resilience that have always been yours. Together, these two forces form the foundation of every strategic move to come. Without them, power remains a distant dream, something to be asked for rather than taken. But with them, everything changes. The game shifts. The battlefield is no longer theirs alone to command. And for the first time in history, the rules are no longer theirs to write.

2
Mapping the Terrain of Oppression

The first rule of war is to understand the battlefield. A warrior who marches onto unfamiliar terrain without knowledge of the landscape is already halfway to defeat. In conventional warfare, this means studying topography, supply lines, and fortifications. In the war women are forced to fight every day, the terrain is less tangible but no less real. It is society itself, shaped by generations of laws, expectations, and narratives that determine how power operates and who is allowed to wield it. The terrain of oppression shifts, but its foundation remains the same, designed to limit movement, trap women in cycles of restriction, and ensure that resistance is costly while compliance offers just enough comfort to make submission seem like the safer option.

The first step in navigating this battlefield is identifying different types of terrain. Some spaces are openly oppressive, where misogyny is explicit, where women's voices are dismissed, and where the glass ceiling is not just invisible but actively reinforced. These are workplaces where men dominate leadership, where harassment is an unspoken norm, where contributions are ignored or stolen. These are legislative bodies where laws are written by men who see women's autonomy as negotiable, where reproductive rights are debated rather than treated as fundamental. These are courts that fail to take violence against women seriously, where archaic precedents place the burden of proof on victims rather than perpetrators. These terrains are dangerous, but their hostility is at least transparent, making them easier to recognize.

Then there are terrains that appear neutral but are laced with hidden pitfalls. These are workplaces that tout diversity initiatives but refuse to address systemic barriers that keep women from advancing. These are schools that tell girls they can be anything while still rewarding boys for leadership and punishing girls for assertiveness. These are media spaces that claim to promote women's empowerment while upholding impossible beauty standards and vilifying ambitious women. These terrains are the most exhausting because their hostility is subtle, forcing women into a constant state of self-doubt, making them question whether the barriers they face are real or imagined. A woman who cannot determine whether she is being oppressed is less likely to fight back.

And then there are supportive terrains, spaces where resistance is possible, where allies exist, where power can be cultivated. These are found in feminist organizations, activist movements, and workplaces where women have broken through and reshaped power structures. They exist in relationships built on mutual respect, in educational institutions that challenge rather than reinforce gender norms, in creative spaces where women tell their own stories rather than serving as props in men's narratives. But these terrains are not guaranteed; they must be built and defended. History has shown that feminist movements often face infiltration, co-optation, or internal collapse when vigilance wanes.

Understanding terrain is not just about recognizing where dangers lie, it is about knowing how to move through them effectively. Hostile terrains require different strategies than neutral or supportive ones. In oppressive environments, direct confrontation can be dangerous. Survival requires a balance of resistance and subterfuge, an ability to assess which battles are worth fighting and which will only cause unnecessary harm. The goal is not to reform these environments from within but to extract what is needed, resources, knowledge, connections, while minimizing risk and planning an exit.

Neutral terrains require a different approach. These are spaces where influence can be gained, where power dynamics can be shifted. Change here is slow and incremental, requiring patience, observation, and careful pressure applied at the right moments. It is about creating cracks in the foundation of oppression without triggering immediate backlash.

Supportive terrains, while safer, come with their own challenges. The biggest mistake women make in these spaces is assuming they will remain safe without effort. Power, once gained, must be maintained. Feminist movements have a history of building resistance spaces only to see them infiltrated or weakened when strategies for long-term sustainability were neglected. These spaces require just as much strategy as hostile ones, as they must be fortified against both external threats and internal fractures.

Social media is its own battlefield, both a powerful tool for women's resistance and a dangerous space for female voices. The digital landscape allows for rapid mobilization, amplification of marginalized voices, and exposure of systemic injustices. But it also comes with unprecedented surveillance, harassment, and coordinated efforts to discredit and silence outspoken women. The terrain here shifts constantly. Algorithms reward controversy, making feminist discourse both highly visible and vulnerable to attack. Some women will use their platforms to challenge power directly, while others will operate strategically, using anonymity, coded language, or private networks. There is no single correct approach, but every woman must decide how to navigate this space without allowing it to consume her.

The terrain of oppression is vast and designed to be disorienting. It keeps women in a state of exhaustion, always reacting rather than moving freely. But knowing the terrain is the first step to controlling it. When women can see patterns, structures, and the ways power flows, they are no longer just moving through the battlefield, they are shaping it. Strategy is about positioning, about knowing where you stand and where you need to go. And once a woman understands the terrain, she is no longer just a participant in the fight. She becomes a force capable of altering the landscape itself.

Oppression adapts to challenges. The structures that once kept women in line, outright bans on voting, property ownership, and financial independence, have largely been dismantled. But oppression does not disappear just because its most blatant forms are removed. Instead, it evolves. Workplaces no longer legally exclude women but still pay them less, promote them less often, and subject them to greater scrutiny. Laws that once explicitly treated women as property have been replaced with economic policies and social pressures that still burden them with the majority of unpaid labor. Misogyny once openly expressed in legislation and media has been repackaged into coded language, women are no longer called weak outright, but they are still dismissed as "too emotional" for leadership, "too aggressive" when they demand power, "too distracted" by family obligations to be trusted with authority. The battlefield has changed, but the war continues.

Understanding this evolution is crucial because it prevents the false sense of security that has stalled many feminist movements in the past. Progress is not linear, and victories are not permanent. Women's rights do not move forward in a straight line; they advance, are pushed back, and must be fought for again in new forms. The rules of engagement shift with every political cycle, every economic downturn, every cultural backlash. Women who assume their rights are secure, who believe the world has permanently changed in their favor, are the most vulnerable to the next wave of regression. Vigilance is not paranoia, it is survival.

One of the greatest deceptions of modern oppression is the illusion of neutrality. Hostile terrain is easy to recognize when it announces itself loudly, when governments strip reproductive rights, when companies openly discriminate, when cultures express contempt for female autonomy without shame. But the most dangerous spaces present themselves as neutral or even progressive while quietly reinforcing the same power imbalances. These are institutions that claim to support gender equality while doing nothing to dismantle the barriers preventing women from advancing. These are politicians who declare themselves allies while voting against every measure that would give women real power. These are men who call themselves feminists but still expect women to carry the emotional labor in relationships, who support women's rights in theory but resist the redistribution of power that real equality demands.

Women who do not recognize this trap risk becoming part of a system designed to keep them in place. But just as some terrains appear neutral but are hostile, others appear hostile but hold opportunities. Some of the greatest feminist victories emerged from seemingly impossible conditions. The labor movements of the early twentieth century, the reproductive rights activists who organized in underground networks before abortion was legalized, the women who fought for civil rights while being excluded from both feminist and racial justice spaces, these were all battles waged in hostile landscapes. But because these women understood the terrain, they found weaknesses, built strategies, and refused to let hostility deter them.

Oppression thrives on women not seeing the battlefield clearly. But once enough women refuse to play by the rules that were designed to keep them losing, the entire landscape begins to shift. Not because it was given to them, but because they took it.

The digital landscape is one of the most complex and unpredictable terrains women must navigate today. Social media has become both a tool of empowerment and a weapon of control. It has given women unprecedented access to platforms where they can speak, organize, and challenge power in ways that were never possible before. It has also become a space where misogyny is amplified, where harassment is weaponized, where women who dare to be visible and outspoken are subjected to levels of scrutiny and abuse that men will never experience.

The terrain of the internet is constantly shifting. Algorithms prioritize content that fuels outrage and division, making feminist discourse both more visible and more vulnerable to attack. The speed of information dissemination creates opportunities for rapid mobilization, but it also makes misinformation and targeted disinformation campaigns more dangerous than ever. Women who navigate this space must be both strategic and adaptable. They must recognize that visibility comes with risks, that the digital terrain can turn hostile in an instant, and that their presence in these spaces must be as deliberate as their actions in the physical world.

Family structures, often assumed to be the most stable and personal of terrains, are another battlefield that many women fail to recognize as such until they find themselves trapped within them. Patriarchy does not just operate in public institutions; it thrives in the private sphere. The expectations placed on daughters, sisters, mothers, and wives are not separate from the larger systems of control, they are reflections of them. The pressure on women to be caregivers, to put family before self, to sacrifice career ambitions for domestic responsibilities, is not just cultural tradition; it is economic and political strategy. A woman burdened with the bulk of household labor is a woman with less time and energy to compete in the workplace, less ability to engage in activism, less freedom to pursue independence. A woman taught from childhood that her role is to nurture and accommodate is a woman less likely to demand equality in her relationships, less likely to recognize coercion and manipulation for what they are. The family unit, when structured around patriarchal expectations, is a tool of control as powerful as any law or policy.

To map the terrain of oppression is to understand that no space is truly neutral. Every environment women move through is shaped by power dynamics, by cultural expectations, by economic forces that are often invisible but deeply felt. Some terrains are outright hostile, demanding resistance at every turn. Others are deceptively safe, encouraging women to lower their guard just enough to keep them from pushing further. And some, though dangerous, hold the possibility for transformation. The key is to recognize them for what they are, to stop assuming that oppression is only found in the most obvious places, to stop mistaking symbols of progress for real change. Women who understand the battlefield are women who cannot be easily manipulated, cannot be pacified with half-measures, cannot be convinced that the fight is over before it has truly begun. The world does not simply become less oppressive on its own. It is forced to change by those who see the terrain clearly and refuse to accept its boundaries as permanent.

The key to survival in any battle is understanding not only the terrain but the forces moving through it. Oppression is not a faceless, shapeless mist; it is a system actively maintained by individuals, institutions, and cultural norms that shift to adapt to threats against their control. Women are taught to believe that the barriers they face are incidental, that the struggles they endure are simply the result of bad luck, poor choices, or individual shortcomings. But the reality is that these barriers are deliberately placed. The obstacles are not accidental; they are systemic. They exist because oppression is an engineered condition, constantly recalibrated to ensure that those in power remain there. The world women navigate is a battlefield where the rules are written to favor the enemy. And just as any strategist must assess the landscape of war, women must assess the structures, players, and traps that define their oppression.

The most obvious structures of oppression exist in legal and economic systems. These are the terrains where patriarchy has fortified itself in laws, policies, and financial systems that determine who has autonomy, who has access to resources, and who remains dependent. Many countries have legal frameworks that appear neutral but function as tools of oppression when examined closely. The criminal justice system, for example, has long been weaponized against women, criminalizing their survival, punishing their self-defense, and deprioritizing their safety. A woman who kills an abusive husband in self-defense is far more likely to receive a harsh sentence than a man who kills his wife in an act of rage.

A woman who reports sexual violence is more likely to have her own history, clothing choices, or credibility put on trial than to see her attacker face real consequences. The gender pay gap is not a myth, nor is it simply a result of individual career choices. It is deliberately maintained through wage suppression, glass ceilings, and occupational segregation that push women into lower-paying, less secure work while keeping the highest-paid, most influential positions in male hands. Even when women break through, they face economic punishments, higher scrutiny, greater emotional labor expectations, and career stagnation due to unpaid caregiving responsibilities.

Oppression is reinforced through culture, media, and everyday interactions, making it harder to recognize. Media normalizes power structures by portraying women as love interests, side characters, or symbols of suffering. Even when women lead stories, they are often written through a male lens, serving men's emotional arcs, being punished for ambition, or redeemed through sacrifice. Female politicians are judged on their likability and clothing, not policies. Women in male-dominated fields are questioned about balancing career and family in ways men never are. Women who speak out are labeled shrill, unreasonable, or ungrateful. These narratives aren't just harmful stereotypes; they are distractions, designed to keep women so focused on proving their worth that they lack time to challenge the systems withholding power.

One of the most dangerous terrains women navigate is the unspoken social expectations dictating their behavior. Women are conditioned to be agreeable, prioritize relationships over ambition, and avoid conflict. These expectations serve to keep women from threatening power. A woman who demands what she deserves is arrogant. A woman who refuses mistreatment is difficult. A woman unapologetic in ambition is dangerous. The punishment for failing to comply is swift, professional isolation, reputational attacks, or outright violence. These are deliberate forms of control, keeping women policing themselves, hesitating before speaking, questioning whether their instincts are valid. A woman who is constantly second-guessing herself is easier to control.

Then there is internalized oppression, the battlefield inside women's own minds, colonized by centuries of conditioning. This is the most insidious terrain, turning women against themselves before they can resist. It is the voice that whispers they are not smart enough, strong enough, deserving enough. The impulse to apologize for taking up space, to defer to male authority even when they know better, to shrink to avoid discomfort. The belief that if they work hard enough, are agreeable enough, they will be rewarded. This is one of patriarchy's most effective weapons, it does not require enforcement; it maintains itself. It keeps women trapped in cycles of self-doubt, ensuring the system does not have to exert control externally because the conditioning does the work.

Understanding these terrains is about learning how to navigate them strategically. Oppression is not an immovable force but a series of calculated mechanisms that can be disrupted. The first step is knowing where the dangers lie. In hostile environments, direct resistance is costly; survival requires subversion, gathering intelligence, forming alliances, leveraging resources, and strategically choosing when to fight back. In neutral spaces, influence can be cultivated, identifying opportunities to shift narratives, challenge norms without immediate retaliation, and create cracks in the foundation of oppression. In supportive spaces, the priority is preservation, maintaining and strengthening the few places where women have control, ensuring they are not infiltrated or dismantled.

And then there is the terrain that does not yet exist, the one women must build. The goal is not merely to navigate oppression but to destroy it, to create new structures and ways of existing not dictated by those who benefit from subjugation. Women who understand oppression do not just survive, they reshape it. They refuse to play by the rules that were written to keep them losing. They stop asking for power and start taking it. They stop waiting for permission to fight and recognize they have been at war all along.

Oppression maintains itself by making its mechanisms invisible. The war against women operates through policy decisions that appear neutral but disproportionately harm women, through cultural narratives that normalize male dominance, through economic structures that ensure financial dependency while telling women they are responsible for their own success. Women who complain are told they are imagining things, being too sensitive, that if they just worked harder, they would succeed. But the rules were never designed to serve them, they were designed to keep them proving themselves, chasing equality that remains out of reach.

This terrain forces women to play two roles: competitors in a world that does not want them to win and caretakers in a world that expects them to prioritize others over themselves. Women are asked to be leaders but not too aggressive, to speak up but remain pleasant, to be ambitious but not at the expense of relationships. The contradiction is intentional. If women are too accommodating, they are seen as weak. If they are too assertive, they are seen as unlikeable. There is no right way to move through this terrain without consequence, and that is the point.

Women are conditioned to see one another as competition rather than allies. The system benefits from division, keeping women navigating internal conflicts instead of dismantling the structures that created them. Patriarchy thrives when women distrust one another, when they are convinced that success requires distancing themselves from other women rather than working collectively to shift power. This is why female friendships are dismissed as frivolous while male networking is seen as strategic. It is why older women who fought for their place in male-dominated industries sometimes resist making space for younger women, fearing their hard-earned positions will be threatened. The scarcity model was not created by women, but it has been effective in keeping them divided.

Oppression is reinforced in intimate spaces, families, relationships, and social circles. The expectation that women will always compromise, manage emotions, and maintain harmony is unpaid labor that keeps them too drained to challenge systems benefiting from their exhaustion. The same societies that tell women they can be anything still expect them to handle household duties, child-rearing, and emotional labor, even as they work full-time jobs. When women push back, they meet resistance, not just from men, but from women who have internalized the belief that their worth is tied to sacrifice.

Even in spaces claiming to support women, the terrain remains fraught. Feminism is often co-opted, reduced to a marketable aesthetic instead of a radical movement for systemic change. Brands use feminism to sell products, politicians use it for votes, corporations use it to appear progressive while continuing to exploit female employees.

Women are encouraged to be confident, but these messages do not come with policy changes that guarantee maternity leave, protect against workplace discrimination, or make childcare affordable. They do not come with economic reforms addressing that single mothers are more likely to live in poverty, that women's pensions are smaller because they are expected to take time off to care for children and aging parents, that female-dominated industries remain underpaid. The system is happy to tell women to be strong, so long as that strength does not come with demands for real change.

Mapping this terrain is about recognizing oppression's adaptability, seeing how power disguises itself, how resistance is neutralized before it gains momentum. No victory is permanent. Every gain must be protected. The fight does not end just because the most obvious barriers are removed. Women who understand this landscape do not waste time debating whether sexism still exists. They do not wait for permission to challenge power. They see the patterns, how history repeats, how backlash follows progress. And because they see it, they are prepared.

The battlefield is not fair, but it is not unchangeable. Oppression thrives on women not seeing the battlefield clearly. But once enough refuse to play by rules meant to keep them losing, the entire landscape begins to shift. Not because it was given to them, but because they took it.

3
Strategic Patience and Timing

Timing is everything in war, and it is everything in the battle against oppression. Sun Tzu understood that victory is rarely achieved by sheer force alone but by knowing when to strike and when to wait. He saw that battles are won long before they begin, determined not by who is strongest in the moment but by who has positioned themselves most effectively over time. This principle is just as crucial in the struggles women face today. Oppression does not collapse overnight, and resistance movements do not succeed by acting impulsively. Strategy is not just about action, it is about patience, about recognizing when the conditions are right, about ensuring that every move is deliberate and every confrontation is winnable.

Too often, women are expected to rush into battle, to demand change immediately, to expend all their energy on a single push, only to be met with exhaustion, backlash, and the slow realization that the enemy they are fighting has already anticipated their moves. Power structures rely on women's frustration, on their urgency, on their belief that change must come quickly or not at all. But real victories, lasting victories, come from playing the long game.

Patience is not inaction; it is preparation. It is studying the enemy, understanding their weaknesses, gathering resources, and waiting until the moment is right. Oppression is sustained through endurance, through a system that can outlast fleeting moments of rebellion. The structures that uphold inequality are designed to withstand bursts of outrage, to absorb protests and calls for change without actually changing. They offer small concessions, temporary reforms, distractions meant to pacify dissent before it can build momentum. This is why so many movements have been silenced before achieving their true goals, because they expended everything too soon, believing that moral urgency alone would be enough to shift the balance of power. But the enemy does not operate on urgency. The enemy operates on control, on attrition, on ensuring that those who oppose them run out of steam before they run out of power. The solution is not to fight harder; it is to fight smarter.

Women throughout history have understood this, even if they have not always been credited for it. The suffragists did not win the right to vote by demanding it once and giving up when they were ignored. They studied the opposition, identified weak points, built coalitions, used the media to shape public perception, and forced the hand of those in power by making it politically and socially impossible to deny them. The civil rights movement, the labor movement, the fight for reproductive rights, none of these battles were won in a single moment. They were won through years, sometimes decades, of persistence, through well-timed actions that were impossible to ignore. Rosa Parks' refusal to give up her seat was not an impulsive act, it was a strategic decision, planned and executed at precisely the right time to have maximum impact. The #MeToo movement did not emerge from nowhere; it was the result of years of survivors speaking out, of legal cases being fought, of cultural shifts that had been building below the surface. Every victory that seems sudden is actually the result of careful groundwork laid by those who understood that timing is the difference between failure and success.

Yet women are rarely encouraged to think in terms of long-term strategy. They are expected to react, to respond, to fight for their rights the moment they are threatened, but without the luxury of preparation or the power of sustained pressure.

This is by design. Women who act out of desperation are easier to dismiss. Women who protest without structure are easier to ignore. Women who demand change without leverage are easier to deny. The world does not fear women's outrage, it fears their patience. It fears the moment women stop reacting and start planning, the moment they stop fighting every small battle and instead focus on dismantling the system piece by piece. This is what strategic patience offers, the ability to choose battles wisely, to understand that some fights are meant to be endured rather than won outright, that some concessions are traps meant to stall momentum, that some defeats are necessary in order to win a larger war.

The difficulty, of course, is that patience is hard when injustice is immediate. It is hard to wait when rights are being stripped away, when opportunities are being denied, when violence is happening in real time. But waiting does not mean accepting. It means building, preparing, strengthening alliances, and ensuring that when action is taken, it is not merely symbolic but transformative. It means recognizing the difference between reaction and revolution. It means refusing to be provoked into battles that will only drain resources without shifting power. Every oppressive system thrives on exhaustion, on making resistance feel futile, on making women believe that if they do not act now, they will lose everything. But rushing into a battle unprepared is what ensures defeat. This is not about hesitation. It is about mastery. It is about ensuring that when a move is made, it is unstoppable.

Strategic patience does not mean silence. It does not mean inaction. It does not mean accepting oppression as inevitable. It means choosing the terms of engagement. It means seeing beyond the immediate crisis and preparing for the larger war. It means recognizing that sometimes the most powerful action is restraint, that sometimes the strongest move is the one that is not made until the conditions are right. This is how real change happens, not through bursts of outrage that fade as quickly as they rise, but through pressure that does not let up, through movements that cannot be co-opted, through demands that do not dissolve into compromises that only preserve the status quo.

Women have been conditioned to believe that their power lies in their ability to endure, to adapt, to make the best of a system that refuses to serve them. But endurance is not enough. Adaptation is not enough. Winning requires knowing when to push and when to pull back, when to strike and when to wait, when to demand and when to build until the demand cannot be denied. This is what Sun Tzu understood, that victory is not about fighting every battle but about knowing which battles matter, about choosing engagements that weaken the enemy while strengthening oneself. It is about understanding that oppression is not static, that it shifts and reforms itself in response to resistance, that every victory is met with a counterattack meant to reclaim the lost ground.

Strategic patience means refusing to be baited into unwinnable fights. It means recognizing when power is offering meaningless concessions to pacify rather than transform. It means refusing to be placated by gestures that do not shift real power. It means understanding that lasting change is built over time, through persistence, through moments of silence as much as through moments of action. It means knowing that a battle lost today may be necessary for a war won tomorrow. The world is used to women demanding justice in the moment, it is not prepared for women planning, waiting, and striking only when they cannot be ignored.

This chapter is not about telling women to wait indefinitely. It is about ensuring that when they move, they move with force, with strategy, with preparation that makes their victory inevitable. It is about recognizing that oppression relies on their exhaustion, on their willingness to burn out before the system does. It is about shifting from reaction to revolution, from outrage to orchestration, from fighting for survival to fighting for complete transformation. Because the battle is not just about resisting oppression, it is about ending it. And that requires not just fighting, but winning.

The most effective movements in history were not those that fought constantly but those that fought strategically. The Montgomery Bus Boycott was not spontaneous, it was carefully planned for over a year, requiring coordination, financial support, and the patience to withstand setbacks. The women's suffrage movement did not succeed because women merely protested loudly; it succeeded because they adapted their tactics, built alliances, and recognized when to apply pressure and when to retreat. The #MeToo movement did not explode overnight, it was built on decades of legal battles, grassroots organizing, and cultural shifts that made its impact inevitable when the moment arrived. This is what strategic patience means, not waiting passively for justice, but working beneath the surface, ensuring that when the time comes, the system has no choice but to yield.

Women have often been forced into reactionary roles, responding to crises rather than shaping the conditions that prevent crises from occurring. This is not a reflection of their lack of strategy but of the nature of oppression itself. Systems of power force those they subjugate to remain in survival mode, to stay so busy putting out fires that they never have time to build something stronger. The cycle repeats itself, each generation of women fighting the same battles, demanding the same rights, exhausted before they have the chance to think beyond immediate resistance. The enemy relies on this. Oppressive structures are designed to outlast moments of defiance, absorbing resistance without being fundamentally changed. They expect women to burn out, to move on, to become discouraged, to settle for partial victories rather than full transformations. The antidote to this is not just persistence, it is precision.

Women must move beyond reacting to injustices as they arise and begin dismantling the systems that make those injustices inevitable. This requires a shift in thinking, from short-term protest to long-term strategy. Outrage alone will not change the world, and neither will hope. What changes the world is relentless, deliberate, calculated action, choosing battles wisely, targeting weaknesses in the system rather than throwing energy into fights designed to exhaust. Strategic patience means recognizing that some demands will not be met today, not because they are impossible, but because the conditions for success have not yet been created. It means recognizing that sometimes winning requires stepping back, gathering strength, and striking when the enemy is at its most vulnerable.

Oppressive structures do not simply give up power when asked. They calculate their own moves, adjusting their tactics in response to resistance. This is why progress often feels like running in place, each time women achieve a victory, the system finds a new way to undermine it. Women gain access to the workplace, but the wage gap remains. Women earn legal rights, but enforcement mechanisms remain weak. Women speak out against harassment, but retaliation ensures they lose their jobs instead of their abusers. These patterns are not coincidences; they are deliberate recalibrations of power. The only way to counter them is with an equal level of calculation, anticipating backlash, preparing for it, and ensuring that each step forward is not just symbolic but foundational.

One of the key components of strategic patience is understanding that all movements are vulnerable to co-optation. Feminism, for instance, has repeatedly been diluted by corporate interests, turned into a brand rather than a movement for systemic change. Companies will happily market empowerment while continuing to exploit female workers. Politicians will adopt feminist rhetoric while voting against policies that would give women real power. The system is adept at absorbing the language of resistance while ensuring that true change remains out of reach. This is why women must be vigilant, refusing to be satisfied with superficial victories. A woman in a leadership position does not mean the system has changed if that woman is still operating within a framework designed to limit her power. A workplace diversity initiative means nothing if the wage gap persists. A public statement of support for women's rights is meaningless if laws are being passed to strip those rights away. Strategic patience means refusing to be placated by symbolic wins and pushing for structural change, even when it takes longer than expected.

The power of patience is also evident in the way women must navigate hostile environments. Sun Tzu understood that the best warriors do not fight every battle, some battles are won by avoiding them entirely, by maneuvering around the enemy, by allowing the enemy to weaken itself before striking. Women in male-dominated fields understand this intuitively. They know that pushing too hard too soon can lead to backlash, that survival sometimes requires calculated silence, that timing is often the difference between success and failure. This is not submission, it is strategy. It is knowing when to challenge authority and when to observe, when to demand and when to build quiet leverage. Women have historically been forced into spaces where their presence alone is a challenge to power. The ones who have succeeded have often done so not by forcing immediate change but by positioning themselves in ways that made their success undeniable. This is not about accepting injustice; it is about ensuring that resistance is effective rather than performative.

One of the greatest advantages of strategic patience is that it allows movements to build resilience. Reactionary activism burns out quickly, if every issue is treated as an emergency, resources become depleted, morale drops, and movements collapse before they can achieve real change. The most successful revolutions in history were not waged through constant fighting but through sustained, deliberate efforts. The civil rights movement did not win because activists protested every day without rest; it won because they organized, built legal cases, secured funding, trained leaders, and ensured that their efforts could be sustained for years. The fight for gender equality requires the same endurance. It requires women to recognize that while urgency is necessary, it must be paired with sustainability. Change is not measured in moments of outrage but in shifts of power that cannot be undone.

Strategic patience also applies to personal battles. Women are often pressured to prove themselves immediately, to take every opportunity, to never say no, to fight for every inch. But not every battle is worth fighting. Sometimes the best move is to conserve energy, to wait for better opportunities, to recognize when the costs of engagement outweigh the benefits. Women have been conditioned to believe that they must always be doing more, but true power comes from knowing when to do less, when to step back, when to allow the enemy to weaken itself before taking action. This is not passivity; it is mastery.

Oppression is designed to be exhausting. It is built to keep women fighting endless small battles instead of focusing on the larger war. But the moment women start choosing their battles, the moment they start thinking not in terms of immediate demands but in terms of long-term strategy, everything changes. The system is prepared for outrage. It is not prepared for patience. It is not prepared for women who refuse to burn out, who refuse to be manipulated into reactionary cycles, who understand that timing is not just about when to fight, but about when to win.

The world does not fear women's anger; it fears their planning. It fears the moment women stop asking for change and start ensuring that change is inevitable. It fears the moment women stop trying to prove themselves and start building power that cannot be dismissed. This is what strategic patience offers, the ability to move beyond fighting for survival and toward shaping the future. Oppressive systems thrive on exhaustion, but they crumble under persistence. Women who understand this are not just resisting, they are winning. And winning is the only goal that matters.

Strategic patience is not about waiting for permission. It is about waiting for the right moment, the right conditions, the point where pressure will be most effective and resistance most difficult to ignore. This is the difference between movement and momentum. Women have always been moving, pushing against boundaries, challenging expectations, demanding justice. But momentum is different. Momentum happens when movement builds upon itself, when each action strengthens the next, when a shift becomes inevitable rather than aspirational. Oppressive systems know how to handle isolated acts of resistance. They know how to absorb them, how to let the storm pass without changing the structure. What they fear is sustained pressure, resistance that is not only strong but disciplined, movements that do not just react to injustice but anticipate and counter it with precision.

This is why the most effective uprisings are those built over time, that gather force like a storm, ensuring that by the time they make impact, there is no option but to change. The fall of apartheid in South Africa, the civil rights movement in the United States, the long struggle for women's suffrage, none of these were won through a single moment of protest. They were won through careful organization, years of strategic action, deliberate application of pressure in ways that those in power could not ignore or suppress. Every movement that has succeeded in shifting the balance of power did so not because people simply demanded change, but because they made change inevitable. This is the goal of strategic patience, not to ask, not to plead, but to build so much power that the system has no choice but to break.

But patience does not mean complacency. The biggest misconception about this strategy is that it requires passivity, that it asks women to wait instead of act. This is exactly what those in power want women to believe. They want women to think that patience means acceptance, that strategy means inaction, that waiting means submission. But this is not the patience of the powerless. It is the patience of the strategist, of those who understand that not every battle is worth fighting, that energy must be conserved for when it matters, that victory is not about fighting every fight but about winning the ones that count. This is the kind of patience that has been used by every major revolutionary movement, by every marginalized group that has overthrown its oppressors. It is not about waiting to be handed justice. It is about making justice impossible to deny.

One of the most powerful aspects of strategic patience is its ability to disrupt the expected patterns of power. Oppressive systems are built on predictability. They expect women to respond in certain ways, to fight back when provoked, to burn out when exhausted, to turn against each other when resources are scarce. They have built mechanisms for absorbing outrage, redirecting resistance into endless cycles of conflict that change nothing. But when women break these patterns, when they refuse to play the expected role, when they step back instead of rushing forward, when they gather their forces rather than depleting them, the system falters. It does not know how to counter a strategy it cannot predict. It does not know how to defend against an opponent that does not act out of desperation but out of calculated purpose.

Women have been conditioned to believe that the only way to gain power is to constantly prove themselves, to work harder, to push harder, to always be doing more. But true power does not come from exhaustion. It comes from control. It comes from knowing when to act and when to hold back. It comes from refusing to be baited into unwinnable fights. Oppressive systems count on women's urgency. They count on the belief that if something is not fought for immediately, it will be lost forever. This is how they maintain control, by keeping women in a constant state of reactive struggle, ensuring they are too drained to ever mount a real offensive. But the moment women refuse to play that game, the rules shift. The moment women stop allowing the system to set the terms of engagement, the system starts to lose its grip.

Look at the movements that have made real, lasting change, and the same pattern appears again and again: discipline, coordination, and an understanding that time can be an ally rather than an enemy. The fight for abortion rights in the United States has not just been about individual cases or singular protests, it has been a decades-long battle, one that has required continuous adaptation, the building of networks, the creation of infrastructure that ensures that even when laws are stripped away, access is still possible. The battle for marriage equality did not begin in the 2000s, it was built on the foundation of decades of legal battles, cultural shifts, and social activism that prepared the ground for its eventual success. Every major feminist victory has been the result of long-term strategy, not just momentary defiance.

This is why the most dangerous women in history have not been those who shouted the loudest but those who built the strongest foundations. Harriet Tubman did not just free enslaved people, she built an underground network that could sustain itself over time, that could continue to function even when individual leaders were targeted. The women behind the suffrage movement did not just demand the right to vote, they created entire political organizations that ensured their fight would continue even as laws and tactics changed. The women who have led revolutions did not just take up arms, they studied their opponents, infiltrated systems of power, positioned themselves so that by the time they struck, there was no possibility of defeat. This is what makes strategic patience so dangerous, it is not just about endurance, but about power. It is about ensuring that the fight is never just about survival, but about total transformation.

And this is the lesson that must be learned now. The world is at a turning point, and women are at the center of it. Every system built to suppress them is showing cracks, every institution that has kept them in place is struggling to maintain control. But moments like this do not last forever. They are opportunities, not guarantees. The difference between a moment of potential and a moment of revolution is strategy. It is the decision to not just fight the battles presented but to choose the battles that matter. It is the ability to look beyond the immediate crisis and build something stronger. Winning does not come from reacting to every injustice but from ensuring that the conditions for justice are unshakable.

The final truth of strategic patience is that it is not just a tool, it is a mindset. It is the ability to see beyond the present, to refuse to be limited by what exists, to understand that time is not something to fear but something to use. Oppression is not inevitable, power is not immutable, and change is not something that happens, it is something that is made. Women who understand this are not just fighting against the world as it is. They are creating the world as it should be. And that is what makes them unstoppable.

The world does not expect women to be patient in this way. It does not expect them to be deliberate, strategic, to choose battles with precision rather than passion alone. But that is what makes this approach powerful. The system is built to withstand anger. It is not built to withstand a slow, methodical dismantling of its foundations. It is not built to withstand women who do not just resist but who plan, calculate, and ensure that every move is one step closer to the final collapse of the structures that have held them back for too long. And that is the future that awaits. Not just resistance. Not just survival. But victory. Not because it is given, not because it is begged for, but because it is taken, patiently, deliberately, and with the full knowledge that those who understand timing will always win in the end.

4
Divide and Conquer the Patriarchy

Patriarchal systems are not invincible. They function by projecting an illusion of unity, strength, and inevitability, but beneath the surface, they are riddled with fractures, contradictions, and internal conflicts. These systems are upheld not just by those who directly benefit from them but also by those who fear the consequences of stepping outside them, those who have been conditioned to accept their place within the hierarchy, and those who, despite their suffering under patriarchy, still find reasons to defend it. Divide and conquer is not just a strategy used by oppressive systems, it is a strategy that can be used against them. The same forces that patriarchy has wielded to suppress opposition, fear, division, and manufactured loyalty, can be turned back on it, exploited to accelerate its collapse. This is not about creating chaos for its own sake. It is about understanding the fault lines within patriarchy, recognizing where its defenders are weakest, and applying pressure in ways that fracture their cohesion rather than exhausting the opposition.

One of the most effective ways to weaken patriarchal power is to exploit its reliance on false unity. Patriarchy does not function as a singular, seamless entity. It is a network of institutions, cultural narratives, economic structures, and political alliances that often operate in contradiction with one another. Conservative religious institutions, for example, demand rigid gender roles and submission from women, while corporate capitalism, another pillar of patriarchy, relies on women's labor, both paid and unpaid, to sustain itself. These contradictions create vulnerabilities. The same men who advocate for strict gender roles also benefit from the economic independence of women who contribute to household incomes, from the caregiving labor that keeps workplaces functioning, and from the consumer market driven by female spending. The same corporations that market "empowerment" to women still maintain wage gaps, glass ceilings, and systemic bias. These tensions create pressure points, and pressure points create opportunities.

One of the clearest ways patriarchy maintains its dominance is through fear, fear of change, fear of losing status, fear of the consequences of rebellion. Women are conditioned to fear the repercussions of stepping outside traditional roles. They are told they will be unsafe without male protection, that they will be alone if they reject marriage and family, that their worth is tied to male approval. Men, too, are conditioned by fear, fear of losing control, of being outperformed by women, of having to confront their own complicity in an unjust system. These fears are leveraged to enforce patriarchal norms, ensuring that even those who suffer under patriarchy continue to uphold it. But fear is not just a tool of control, it is also a weakness. When people are ruled by fear, they are prone to overreaction, to division, to internal conflict that can be used against them.

Exposing and amplifying these internal conflicts is a powerful way to weaken patriarchal power structures. There are already deep divisions within male-dominated spaces, between conservative traditionalists who want to maintain rigid gender roles and more progressive men who believe in at least partial equality, between corporate elites who see women as an economic asset and reactionary politicians who see them as a threat to traditional power, between men who exploit women and those who believe they are protecting them. These divisions are often obscured by a common enemy, feminism, social progress, the shifting balance of power. But when these fractures are exposed and deepened, patriarchal forces begin to turn on each other. When men are forced to confront the fact that their allies are also their competitors, when institutions that have always worked together begin to realize their interests are not truly aligned, the system starts to weaken.

One of the greatest weapons patriarchy has used against
women is the division between them. The system has relied on
turning women against each other, fostering competition,
jealousy, and distrust. White women were historically pitted
against Black and Indigenous women, encouraged to see
themselves as superior allies of male power rather than victims
of the same structures. Professional women were told that
feminism was about individual success rather than collective
liberation, leading to a version of "empowerment" that left
working-class women behind. Mothers were positioned against
child-free women, married women against single women,
older women against younger women. These divisions were
not accidental. They were deliberately cultivated to prevent
women from forming the kind of unified front that would pose
a real threat to patriarchal power.

Reversing this tactic requires deliberately fostering solidarity.
It requires rejecting the idea that there is only one way to be a
feminist, that there is only one way to fight oppression, that
some women's struggles are more valid than others. It means
acknowledging that while all women experience patriarchy,
they do not experience it in the same way. Race, class,
sexuality, disability, and economic status all shape the ways in
which women are affected by oppression, and ignoring these
differences only serves to deepen divisions. The solution is not
to pretend that all women are the same but to build coalitions
that recognize and respect these differences while focusing on
shared goals. The goal is not unity for its own sake, it is
strategic solidarity, alliances that are strong because they
acknowledge complexity rather than erasing it.

Patriarchy is not just upheld by men. Women who have
internalized its values often become its most dedicated
enforcers. There are women who align themselves with male
power in order to gain protection or status. There are women
who attack feminists more viciously than men do, believing
that their compliance will shield them from patriarchy's worst
excesses. There are women who reinforce beauty standards,

who judge other women for their choices, who uphold the very norms that keep them oppressed. These women are often placed in visible positions as proof that patriarchy is not real, after all, if a woman is enforcing the system, how can the system be sexist? But these women are not proof of patriarchy's fairness; they are proof of its adaptability. Patriarchy rewards women who enforce its rules, who uphold its hierarchies, who keep other women in line. But they are also expendable. The same system that rewards them will discard them the moment they cease to be useful.

Recognizing this does not mean giving up on these women as potential allies, it means understanding that alliances must be built on shared interests, not just shared identity. There are women who enforce patriarchy because they believe it benefits them, but there are also women who enforce it out of fear, out of conditioning, out of the belief that there is no alternative. Some will never change. Some will. The key is knowing where to invest energy, when to engage and when to walk away, when to challenge and when to focus on building power elsewhere. Time spent trying to convince those who are fully committed to patriarchy is often wasted. Time spent strengthening those who are already questioning the system, who are already looking for an alternative, is time well spent.

Coalition-building is not about seeking approval from the existing power structure, it is about creating a new power structure that does not rely on their permission. This means not only uniting women but also building alliances with men and nonbinary people who understand that patriarchy harms them too. There are men who see how rigid gender roles limit their humanity, who want to be free from the expectations of dominance and emotional repression. There are nonbinary and gender-nonconforming people who are targeted by patriarchy even more aggressively than women, who have always been a threat to the rigid categories patriarchy depends on. These allies are not just useful, they are essential. The goal is not just to defeat patriarchy as it exists today but to dismantle the entire structure that allows it to exist at all.

Patriarchy survives not because it is invincible but because it is adaptable. It shifts, rebrands, and recalibrates to maintain control, exploiting divisions to weaken opposition and absorbing resistance into forms that do not threaten its power. It does not hold its power through brute force alone but through psychological manipulation, ensuring that even those it oppresses become its defenders. This is why women who resist patriarchy often find themselves facing not just men but other women who have been conditioned to uphold the same system.

It is why social movements fracture over seemingly small ideological differences, why feminist organizations have historically struggled to remain unified, why each wave of feminism has been met not only with backlash from men but also with skepticism from women who question its priorities. Patriarchy understands that a divided opposition is an ineffective one, and it has mastered the art of playing different groups against one another. The key to dismantling this system is not just in resisting it directly but in ensuring that its own tactics are used against it, forcing it to confront the very divisions it has used to maintain its power.

One of the most effective ways to weaken patriarchy is to expose the internal contradictions that it depends on. It presents itself as a natural order, as an ancient and unshakable foundation of human society, but in reality, it is a patchwork of competing ideologies, shifting economic interests, and contradictory moral codes that often work against one another. It is not a unified force but a coalition of convenience, held together by the shared goal of maintaining male dominance but divided over how best to do so. Religious conservatives insist that women's primary role is in the home, while capitalist institutions rely on women's labor in the workplace. Some men defend chivalry and male protectionism, while others champion unrestrained male aggression and dominance. Some patriarchal ideologues argue that women are weak and fragile, while others insist that women are cunning manipulators who secretly control the world. These contradictions exist because patriarchy does not operate on truth but on power, bending its justifications to suit the needs of the moment. The goal is not to point out these contradictions in the hope that patriarchy will recognize its own hypocrisy, because it won't, but to use these fractures to drive wedges between its supporters, ensuring that they are too divided to sustain a unified front.

A critical fault line within patriarchy lies between its various male enforcers. The system depends on the loyalty of men to sustain itself, but not all men benefit equally from patriarchy, and not all men enforce it in the same way. There is an undeniable difference between the billionaire who profits from corporate exploitation and the working-class man who struggles under the same economic system that devalues women. There is a difference between the politicians who legislate against women's rights and the men who passively go along with these decisions without fully understanding their impact. Patriarchy maintains its power by convincing men that they all share a common interest, that gender solidarity should outweigh class, race, and political divisions, that feminism is their enemy rather than the economic and political elites who exploit them. But when men begin to recognize that their loyalty to patriarchy benefits only a select few at their expense, cracks begin to form.

This is why patriarchal institutions invest so much effort in keeping men unified under a false sense of shared purpose. They foster the belief that feminism is an attack on men rather than a challenge to an unequal system. They push narratives that frame women's progress as a threat to male stability, convincing working-class men that their struggles are caused by female competition rather than corporate greed, that their declining job prospects are due to affirmative action rather

56

than economic shifts that exploit workers regardless of gender. These are distractions, meant to ensure that men continue to align themselves with the same forces that oppress them.

The solution is not to appeal to patriarchal men in the hopes that they will suddenly recognize the injustice of the system but to encourage them to see where their real enemies are. When men begin to understand that their economic struggles are the result of a system that treats them as disposable laborers just as it treats women as disposable caregivers, when they recognize that their frustrations are being redirected toward women instead of toward the billionaires and policymakers who actually control their lives, patriarchy's ability to maintain itself through false unity begins to collapse.

The same strategy must be applied to women who enforce patriarchy. It is not enough to simply condemn them for their complicity; it is necessary to understand why they uphold the system and where their interests diverge from the men they align themselves with. Many of the women who defend patriarchal values do so not out of genuine belief but out of survival. They recognize, consciously or unconsciously, that aligning with male power offers them protection, status, or stability that they may not have access to otherwise.

A woman who reinforces rigid gender norms may do so because she has been rewarded for doing so. A woman who shames other women for not prioritizing motherhood over career may do so because she was told her worth depended on her ability to conform. A woman who defends sexist policies may do so because she has been made to believe that if she stands with men, she will be spared the worst effects of misogyny. But patriarchy does not ultimately serve these women, it uses them. The moment they are no longer useful, they are discarded. The moment they age out of desirability, out of fertility, out of compliance, they are treated with the same contempt as the women they once judged.

This is a vulnerability that can be exploited. Women who have internalized patriarchal values may not immediately abandon them, but when they begin to see that their compliance does not grant them lasting security, when they begin to witness how quickly the system turns against them, their loyalty weakens. The goal is not to expect immediate transformation but to plant doubt, to allow the contradictions to reveal themselves over time. The more women begin to see that patriarchy is not a guarantee of protection but a trap, the less willing they will be to defend it. This is why feminist movements must resist the temptation to waste energy attacking every woman who upholds patriarchal norms and instead focus on where alliances can be built, where the seeds of doubt can be planted, where the fractures can be widened.

The final and perhaps most important strategy in dividing and conquering patriarchy is coalition-building. The system maintains its power by ensuring that marginalized groups remain divided, that feminists, labor movements, racial justice advocates, and LGBTQ+ activists see themselves as separate fights rather than interconnected struggles against the same oppressive structures. Patriarchy is not just about gender, it intersects with capitalism, white supremacy, and authoritarianism. It depends on division not just between men and women but between different groups of women, between people of different races, classes, and sexual orientations. The most effective way to weaken it is to reject these divisions, to create alliances that recognize the shared roots of oppression while still respecting the unique struggles that different groups face.

Coalition-building does not mean ignoring differences. It does not mean pretending that all struggles are identical or that all solutions are the same. It means recognizing that while the experiences of oppression may differ, the forces behind them are connected. It means ensuring that feminist movements do not replicate the same hierarchies they seek to dismantle, that working-class struggles recognize the unpaid labor of women, that racial justice movements address the unique forms of oppression faced by women of color. It means refusing to let patriarchy dictate the terms of engagement, refusing to be distracted by the infighting that weakens movements, refusing to allow the system to set the rules of the game.

Patriarchy has survived by keeping its enemies divided, by ensuring that those who should be fighting together are instead fighting each other. But when those divisions are exposed, when its contradictions are forced into the open, when the false sense of unity that sustains it is shattered, the system begins to crumble. The goal is not just to challenge patriarchy's power but to ensure that it no longer has the ability to hold itself together. And once that happens, once its foundations begin to crack, the collapse is inevitable.

Patriarchy has relied on its ability to evolve, shifting its justifications, tactics, and alliances to maintain control. It absorbs and repackages opposition, coopting language and narratives to preserve its dominance. It tells women they are equal while ensuring they remain underpaid, overworked, and subject to the whims of male-dominated institutions. It allows token progress, women CEOs, politicians, cultural icons, while keeping the broader structures of power intact. It markets feminism as individual success rather than collective liberation, convincing women that breaking a glass ceiling is more important than dismantling the system that built it. It pits progress against stability, telling women they can fight for their rights, but not too loudly, not too aggressively, not in a way that makes those in power uncomfortable. Patriarchy is a system that thrives on co-optation, on illusion, on ensuring that its control remains even when it appears to be shifting.

This is why dividing and conquering the patriarchy must be done deliberately, strategically, in ways that force its contradictions into the open and dismantle its ability to regroup. The system survives because it convinces people that the enemy is not patriarchy itself, but those fighting against it.

Women are told that feminism is a threat to family stability, to morality, to cultural heritage. Men are told that gender equality is a zero-sum game, that any gain for women is a loss for them. Marginalized communities are pitted against one another, convinced that the struggle for women's rights is separate from the fight against racial injustice, economic exploitation, and systemic inequality. These divisions are the foundation upon which patriarchy maintains itself, and they are also its greatest weakness.

The first step in dismantling patriarchy's false unity is exposing how it serves only a select few. The vast majority of men do not benefit from patriarchy in the way they are led to believe. While they may enjoy certain privileges, the system is ultimately designed to serve the wealthiest, the most powerful, those who sit at the top of the hierarchy while ensuring that all others remain locked in place. Working-class men who buy into patriarchal narratives are not rewarded with power but are instead used as foot soldiers to protect the interests of the elite. They are convinced that their frustrations are the fault of women entering the workforce, rather than the corporations that exploit them. They are told that feminism is why they feel alienated, rather than the economic structures that devalue them as workers and human beings. This is one of patriarchy's most effective illusions: keeping men too focused on maintaining dominance over women to realize they are being dominated themselves.

The men who benefit most from patriarchy, the billionaires, the political elite, the media moguls, will never willingly dismantle it. But men lower in the hierarchy can be persuaded to recognize that their interests do not align with those at the top. This does not mean centering men in feminist struggles; it means breaking the myth that feminism is their enemy. It means ensuring that men understand that fighting patriarchy does not mean losing power, but rather reclaiming the parts of themselves that patriarchy has suppressed, emotional depth, vulnerability, authentic relationships, the ability to exist outside of rigid gender roles that demand domination over others. It means recognizing that patriarchy does not just oppress women, it dehumanizes everyone.

At the same time, dividing patriarchy from within also requires addressing the women who uphold it. Women have always played a role in maintaining patriarchal structures, whether as enforcers of traditional gender roles, as political actors who serve the interests of male power, or as cultural figures who reinforce narratives of compliance. The existence of women within systems of power is often used as evidence that patriarchy is no longer an issue, if women can be CEOs, if women can run for office, if women can hold authority, then surely the fight is over. But this ignores the reality that a handful of women succeeding within patriarchal structures does not mean those structures have been dismantled. In many cases, these women are allowed to rise precisely because they pose no real threat to the system. They are selected because they are willing to uphold the existing order rather than challenge it.

Their presence is used as proof that gender inequality is solved while ensuring that the majority of women remain without real power. The danger of this illusion is that it convinces people that feminism has already won, that the struggles of the past are no longer relevant, and that women who continue to fight for systemic change are unreasonable, ungrateful, or unwilling to recognize their supposed progress. But one woman at the top of a patriarchal structure does not undo the oppression of millions of women beneath her. Representation alone is not liberation.

This does not mean that every woman in a position of power is complicit in patriarchy, but it does mean recognizing the difference between representation and transformation. A woman in power who enforces the same policies that harm women is not a victory. A woman who gains wealth while millions of other women remain in poverty is not a symbol of progress. Feminism that only benefits the privileged is not feminism, it is patriarchy's way of adapting to survive. The goal is not simply to place women into the existing power structures but to change the structures themselves.

This requires confronting and challenging the women who have aligned themselves with patriarchal power, not out of personal hatred but because their role in upholding the system is a strategic liability to feminist movements. Some of these women may be reached through education, exposure, or the gradual realization that their loyalty to patriarchy does not guarantee them security. Others will cling to the system until it no longer serves them. The key is not to waste energy trying to save those who are fully invested in patriarchy but to focus on empowering those who are beginning to question it.

Patriarchy also depends on using identity politics as a tool of division. It tells women that feminism is a white woman's movement, that gender issues are separate from racial or economic struggles, that to fight for one's own liberation is to abandon solidarity with others. It tells Black women that feminism is not for them, that they must choose between racial justice and gender justice, as if the two can be separated. It tells working-class women that feminism is a luxury of the elite, that economic survival must come first. It tells LGBTQ+ activists that their struggles are unrelated to feminist struggles, even though both are about dismantling rigid gender roles and oppressive systems of power.

These divisions are not accidental. They are deliberately cultivated to ensure that each movement remains too fractured to challenge the system in a unified way. The more fragmented the opposition, the easier it is for patriarchy to remain in control. This is why intersectionality is not just a theoretical framework, it is a necessary strategy for survival. It is the recognition that all forms of oppression are interconnected and that no movement can succeed if it refuses to acknowledge the struggles of those who are most marginalized.

The response to this must be coalition-building that is intentional and intersectional. Feminism cannot afford to replicate the same exclusions and hierarchies that patriarchy has enforced. It must actively work to dismantle racism, classism, ableism, and other forms of oppression within its own ranks. It must recognize that the fight against patriarchy is not just a fight for women but a fight against all systems of domination and control. This does not mean erasing differences in experience or pretending that all struggles are identical, but it does mean refusing to let those differences be used as weapons to weaken the movement.

It means recognizing that true solidarity does not come from ignoring privilege but from using privilege to challenge oppression, from ensuring that the most marginalized voices are heard, from building movements that do not just seek small reforms but a fundamental restructuring of power itself. Coalition-building is difficult work, requiring patience, trust, and a willingness to listen. But when done correctly, it creates movements that cannot be easily divided, movements that can withstand the inevitable backlash and co-optation efforts that patriarchy will deploy in response.

Patriarchy has always survived by keeping its opposition divided, by ensuring that those who should be allies see each other as competitors, by turning struggles for justice into battles over limited resources. It has convinced women to fight one another rather than fight the system. It has convinced men that their masculinity is threatened by equality rather than by the rigid roles that have been forced upon them. It has convinced marginalized groups that they must struggle separately rather than together. But when these divisions are exposed for what they are, tools of control rather than natural boundaries, the entire system begins to weaken. The most dangerous thing to patriarchy is not just resistance but coordinated resistance. It is not just individual defiance but collective action. It is the recognition that the divisions patriarchy enforces are its greatest vulnerability, and once those divisions are dismantled, its power begins to crumble. This requires a shift in thinking, from seeing oppression as a series of isolated injustices to understanding it as an interconnected system that must be taken down as a whole. It requires seeing beyond temporary victories and building long-term strategies that ensure permanent change.

Divide and conquer is a strategy that has been used against women, against workers, against marginalized communities for centuries. Now it must be used against the system that created it. The goal is not just to resist patriarchy but to ensure that it can no longer hold itself together. The goal is not just to challenge its power but to make it impossible for it to reassemble in the same form again. Once patriarchy is forced to fight itself, once its internal fractures are widened beyond repair, once those who have been deceived by it recognize their true interests, the entire structure collapses. And that is when real liberation begins.

The fight is not about finding ways to survive within patriarchy but about ensuring that future generations do not have to. It is about creating a world where power is not hoarded but shared, where justice is not conditional, where progress is not measured by how much women can endure but by how much they can build. And for that to happen, patriarchy must be divided and dismantled until it can no longer reassemble itself. This is the true meaning of divide and conquer, not to weaken the opposition but to break the system that has held them in place for far too long.

5
The Element of Surprise

Oppression thrives on predictability. It survives because it assumes those who fight against it will do so in ways that are expected, ways that have been countered before, ways that can be absorbed into the system without actually threatening its existence. Protests are anticipated. Outrage is managed. The system has built entire industries around controlling and defusing resistance, media narratives that discredit activists, legal loopholes that criminalize dissent, economic pressures that force people into compliance.

But what oppression cannot easily handle is the unexpected. It does not know what to do with satire that undermines its authority, with humor that exposes its absurdity, with creative tactics that disrupt its power in ways it did not foresee. This is why the element of surprise is one of the most powerful weapons available to those who oppose injustice. A well-timed, subversive act of resistance does more than challenge power, it forces it into a position where it must either overreact and expose itself or remain silent and lose control of the narrative.

Creativity has always been a tool of revolution, not simply as a means of expression but as a strategy for dismantling the structures that enforce oppression. Throughout history, those who have challenged power most effectively have done so not just through direct confrontation but through subversion, by using art, literature, humor, and unexpected tactics to shift public perception and destabilize the legitimacy of the system they fought against.

The women's suffrage movement did not only march and protest; it used strategic propaganda, political theater, and disruptive tactics that made it impossible to ignore. The civil rights movement did not just stage sit-ins and marches; it used music, fashion, and cultural influence to shift the moral conversation in ways that legal arguments alone could not. The fight against apartheid in South Africa was not only waged in courts and on the streets; it was fought in underground newspapers, in coded songs, in the deliberate use of language that carried hidden meanings only those within the movement could understand. The most successful resistance movements have always been those that understood that power is not just about laws and institutions but about culture, and that to truly undermine an oppressive system, its cultural dominance must be attacked as well.

This is where humor, satire, and absurdity become such effective weapons. Oppressive systems rely on the illusion of authority, on the belief that they are too powerful, too serious, too inevitable to be challenged. But the moment they are laughed at, the moment their contradictions are exposed through humor, the moment they are turned into something ridiculous rather than fearsome, their power begins to erode. Authoritarian regimes, in particular, fear mockery more than open rebellion because mockery strips them of the control they depend on.

This is why so many totalitarian governments have banned satire, imprisoned comedians, censored artists, because they know that a joke, well-placed and well-timed, can do more to undermine them than a speech ever could. When women use humor to expose the absurdity of misogyny, when they turn patriarchal expectations into something laughable rather than intimidating, they shift the balance of power in ways that are difficult to counter.

One of the most effective examples of this is the way feminists have reclaimed and repurposed sexist language. Words that were once used as slurs—"bitch," "nasty woman," "slut,"— have been turned into symbols of power and defiance, stripping them of their ability to be used as weapons of humiliation. The same has been done with expectations around femininity itself. For decades, women were expected to

66

be polite, soft-spoken, accommodating, and in response, feminist movements deliberately embraced the opposite, loudness, anger, refusal to conform.

Movements like Riot Grrrl in the 1990s used punk music and zines to challenge the idea that women had to be quiet to be respected. Social media campaigns today have done the same, using humor and irony to mock the idea that women owe men their time, attention, or obedience. When women refuse to take misogyny seriously, when they turn it into a joke, when they highlight its contradictions, when they mock the men who enforce it, they rob it of its ability to control them.

Art, in all its forms, has also been one of the most powerful tools for resistance. Visual art, literature, music, film, all of these have been used to expose oppression, to rewrite narratives, to challenge the way history is told. Feminist art movements have always understood this. The Guerrilla Girls, for example, used masked anonymity and street art to call out sexism in the art world, forcing major institutions to confront their own biases in ways that direct confrontation had failed to accomplish. Street artists around the world have used public spaces as a battleground, creating murals and installations that make visible the injustices that those in power would prefer to keep hidden.

Even in the digital age, where images and messages can be controlled more tightly than ever, artists and activists find ways to subvert that control, whether through memes that go viral before they can be censored, through guerrilla projection art that turns city buildings into billboards for resistance, or through interactive performances that force audiences to confront their own complicity in oppressive systems. Social media, in particular, has become one of the most effective platforms for creative resistance. Hashtag activism, while sometimes dismissed as performative, has in many cases been a game-changing tool for organizing and mobilizing people around the world. Movements like #MeToo and

#TimesUp were not just about raising awareness, they were about shifting the balance of power, forcing institutions to confront abuses they had previously ignored. The rapid spread of these movements, the way they forced immediate and visible consequences for powerful men, was possible because they used digital platforms in ways that traditional activism had struggled to do.

The same applies to campaigns that use humor and irony to expose misogyny. The "mansplaining" meme culture, which highlights the way men talk over and condescend to women, has done more to make this issue part of mainstream discourse than decades of academic writing on gender dynamics. The phrase "not all men," once used as a defensive argument against feminist critiques, has now become a joke in itself, a shorthand for the refusal of some men to engage in meaningful conversations about gender-based violence. When oppressive behaviors become memes, when they become something so widely mocked that even those who would have previously defended them hesitate, the culture shifts.

Subversive tactics are not just about challenging power directly, they are about rewriting the rules of engagement. Patriarchy expects direct resistance. It is prepared for arguments, for protests, for legal battles. What it struggles to handle is defiance that does not play by its rules, that does not ask for permission, that refuses to engage on the system's terms. It does not know how to control movements that refuse to take it seriously, that refuse to see it as inevitable. This is why creative resistance is so dangerous, it does not seek to engage oppression on its terms, but to make those terms irrelevant.

The most effective acts of creative resistance do not just challenge authority; they force authority into a position where it either exposes its own absurdity or loses control of the conversation. When governments and corporations censor artists, they reveal their own fear. When powerful men complain about being mocked, they reveal their own insecurity. When oppressive systems try to control humor, art, and culture, they reveal that they are losing their grip. This is why creativity is such an essential tool in the fight against patriarchy.

It is not just about expressing resistance; it is about making oppression untenable, about ensuring that the system cannot continue to function as it has. A joke, an artwork, a viral tweet, these may seem like small things, but when used strategically, they are weapons that can change the world. And in a system that depends on control, the ability to surprise, to disrupt, to subvert is one of the most powerful tools of all.

Patriarchy relies on control, control over bodies, over narratives, over the limits of acceptable discourse. It functions by setting boundaries on what can be said, who is allowed to speak, and which ideas are deemed legitimate. It depends on its ability to dictate the terms of debate, ensuring that any challenge to its power must first pass through the very systems it has designed to neutralize opposition.

But creativity refuses to abide by these limits. It does not ask permission, it does not wait for approval, and it does not play by rules that were written to ensure its failure. This is what makes creative and subversive tactics so dangerous to systems of oppression, they operate outside of the traditional frameworks of resistance, using art, humor, and disruption to expose the contradictions and absurdities that patriarchy relies on to maintain control.

One of the most effective aspects of creative resistance is its ability to bypass the mechanisms that power has put in place to silence dissent. Traditional activism, protests, petitions, legal battles, while essential, often takes place within systems that have been built to absorb and deflect these challenges. The media is structured to frame dissent in ways that make it appear unreasonable, aggressive, or impractical. The legal system is designed to slow progress, to exhaust activists with endless delays, to turn justice into a drawn-out war of attrition rather than an urgent demand.

Even public discourse has been shaped to ensure that feminist arguments must constantly be defended against bad-faith attacks, forcing women to repeatedly justify their own humanity rather than pushing forward with the fight for real systemic change. But creative resistance sidesteps these barriers entirely. It does not argue with oppression; it mocks it. It does not debate injustice; it exposes it. It does not play by the rules; it rewrites them.

Satire has long been one of the most effective tools of subversive resistance because it reveals truths that power would prefer to keep hidden. The most dangerous thing about patriarchy is not just its ability to enforce oppression but its ability to normalize it, to convince people that injustice is simply the natural order of things. Satire disrupts this by making oppression visible, stripping it of its disguises, and forcing people to confront its absurdity. When feminists use satire to highlight the hypocrisy of gender roles, when they create parody advertisements that expose the ridiculous expectations placed on women, when they turn misogynistic rhetoric back on itself, they are doing more than just entertaining, they are challenging the very foundations of patriarchy's cultural power.

A sexist politician who can dismiss a protest as irrational or extreme may struggle to respond when his own words are turned into a viral meme that exposes his contradictions. A corporation that profits from exploiting women may find it much harder to maintain its image when feminist artists reimagine its marketing campaigns to reveal the truth behind its empty empowerment rhetoric.

Artistic activism, in all its forms, has the power to reframe narratives in ways that traditional forms of resistance cannot.

Throughout history, feminist artists have used their work to challenge patriarchy not just by confronting it directly, but by creating alternative visions of reality that make its limitations undeniable. The feminist art movement of the 1970s, for example, rejected the male-dominated art world by creating spaces where women's perspectives, experiences, and bodies were centered in ways that mainstream galleries had never allowed.

Artists like Judy Chicago, with her monumental work *The Dinner Party*, rewrote history by giving visibility to the women who had been erased from it. The Guerrilla Girls, through their anonymous public interventions, called out the art world's sexism with brutal, undeniable statistics plastered across major cities. Their work was not just an expression of anger, it was a strategic disruption of an institution that had spent centuries pretending that women's creative voices did not exist. This tradition continues today in new forms, with feminist artists using digital platforms, street art, performance, and public installations to expose the systems that seek to silence them.

Social media has become one of the most powerful tools for subversive feminist activism, not just because of its reach but because it allows women to bypass the traditional gatekeepers of discourse. Historically, women's voices were filtered through male-dominated media institutions, constrained by editorial boards, dependent on approval from the same structures they were trying to challenge. But now, a single tweet, a viral video, or a well-timed meme can dismantle a public figure's credibility, expose a company's hypocrisy, or ignite a global conversation about an issue that had previously been ignored.

The #MeToo movement is a prime example of this, what began as a grassroots digital campaign quickly became an unstoppable force, shifting the cultural landscape in ways that traditional activism had struggled to achieve for decades. The power of #MeToo was not just in its ability to expose individual abusers but in its ability to reshape the narrative around sexual violence, forcing institutions to take action not because they wanted to, but because they could no longer avoid it.

The same principle applies to digital humor as a form of feminist resistance. The rise of feminist meme culture has turned social media into a battleground where misogynistic arguments are dismantled with cutting humor before they even have a chance to take hold. The idea that "women aren't funny" has been obliterated not through serious academic debate but through an avalanche of viral content that proves otherwise. The phrase "not all men," once used as a way to derail conversations about gender-based violence, has been turned into a joke so widely ridiculed that even those who might have once used it now hesitate. This is the power of humor, it shifts the cultural terrain so that certain ideas are no longer seen as worthy of engagement, but as relics of a bygone era that can be laughed out of existence.

Subversion through creativity is not just about messaging; it is about forcing oppressive systems into positions where they can only respond in ways that expose their own weakness. Governments that fear feminist art ban it, revealing their fragility. Corporations that market themselves as allies to women while exploiting their labor are forced to confront public backlash when their hypocrisy is laid bare. Public figures who rely on outdated misogynistic rhetoric become laughingstocks rather than threats when their words are turned into parody. This is why oppressive systems have always sought to control art, to censor satire, to dictate the limits of acceptable discourse, because they know that when people start to see through the illusion of power, when they recognize that they can challenge it not with force but with creativity, the entire foundation of that power begins to crumble.

Creativity in resistance is also about redefining what victory looks like. Too often, movements are told that they must achieve specific legislative or institutional victories to be considered successful. But cultural change precedes political change. Shifting the way people think, the way they talk, the way they engage with the world is just as powerful, if not more so, than any single law or policy. A feminist movement that successfully shifts public perception of gender roles, that makes patriarchal ideas embarrassing rather than dominant, that ensures that young girls grow up seeing themselves as capable, powerful, and deserving of equality, is a movement that has already won. Laws can be changed back. Policies can be repealed. But cultural shifts, once they take hold, are much harder to reverse.

The true power of creative and subversive tactics lies in their ability to make resistance unavoidable. A protest can be ignored. A demand can be dismissed. But a cultural shift, once it begins, seeps into every aspect of life, making it impossible for oppressive systems to function as they once did. Art, humor, digital activism, these are not distractions from the fight against patriarchy. They are the fight itself, because they attack oppression at its roots: in the narratives that sustain it, in the fears that uphold it, in the cultural myths that make it seem inevitable. And once those myths are dismantled, once people can see the absurdity of the structures they were told were unchangeable, the path to real, lasting transformation becomes clear. The revolution does not begin with policy, it begins with imagination, with the refusal to accept the world as it is, and the audacity to create a new one.

Creativity as a tool of resistance is often dismissed because it does not conform to traditional ideas of power. Institutions expect rebellion to look a certain way, organized protests, policy debates, direct legal challenges, because those are the battles they know how to fight. They have spent centuries perfecting the art of deflecting criticism, absorbing dissent, and stalling movements long enough to outlast them. What they do not know how to handle is creativity that refuses to engage on their terms, that rewrites the rules of resistance entirely. Art, humor, and subversive tactics function outside of the conventional frameworks of power, which makes them difficult to control. They create pressure not through demands but through cultural shifts, changing the way people think, feel, and react before institutions even realize what has happened. This is why oppressive systems have always sought to control creative expression, because they understand, even if they do not admit it, that cultural change precedes political change, and that once a shift in perception begins, it is nearly impossible to reverse.

One of the most effective aspects of creative resistance is that it forces oppressive institutions into a no-win situation. When movements use direct confrontation, those in power can respond with brute force, legal maneuvers, or propaganda to delegitimize them. But when movements use humor, satire, or art, they place power in an uncomfortable position. If power ignores it, the message spreads unchallenged, reaching wider audiences and gaining momentum. If power overreacts, censoring art, arresting satirists, publicly condemning humor, it reveals its own insecurity, proving the very point that creative resistance was making in the first place. This has happened countless times throughout history.

In authoritarian regimes, satirists have been imprisoned because their jokes hit too close to the truth. In corporate environments, companies have been forced into damage control after feminist artists reframe their exploitative practices in ways that the public cannot unsee. In politics, leaders who rely on fear and authority have found themselves ridiculed into irrelevance, their power eroded not through force but through laughter.

Satire is particularly powerful because it disrupts the manufactured seriousness that patriarchy and authoritarianism rely on to maintain control. Oppression depends on people believing that the system is too complex, too inevitable, too deeply entrenched to be dismantled. It cultivates an aura of importance, making those who challenge it feel as though they are the ones being unreasonable, as though resistance is an exercise in futility. But satire punctures this illusion, showing that those in power are not untouchable, that their authority is not absolute, that their arguments are often built on contradictions so absurd that they collapse under the weight of their own logic when exposed.

When feminist comedians take misogynistic talking points and exaggerate them to the point of ridiculousness, they are not just making jokes, they are forcing the audience to confront the absurdity of ideas that, when spoken seriously, often go unchallenged. When digital activists create memes that turn oppressive ideologies into punchlines, they are making it more difficult for those ideologies to retain their influence. It is much harder to take an idea seriously once it has been widely mocked, and once people stop taking oppression seriously, it loses a key source of its power: the ability to make itself seem inevitable.

The most effective forms of creative resistance do not just challenge power; they change the conversation entirely. They shift the terms of debate, making old arguments irrelevant before those in power even realize what is happening. This is particularly evident in how feminist movements have reclaimed and redefined language. Historically, patriarchal societies have used language as a weapon, controlling how women are described, how they are allowed to speak, and how they are permitted to frame their own experiences. Women who challenge power are labeled "hysterical," "angry," "difficult."

Women who express sexuality outside of prescribed norms are called "sluts" and "whores." Women who refuse to conform are painted as "unnatural" or "unfeminine." But feminist movements have turned these labels back on patriarchy, stripping them of their intended power. "Nasty woman," meant as an insult, became a badge of honor. "Bossy," once used to silence young girls, has been reclaimed as a sign of leadership. Slut walks, originally designed to protest victim-blaming in cases of sexual violence, took a word meant to shame women and turned it into a symbol of defiance. These linguistic shifts are not just about reclaiming words; they are about dismantling the power structures that those words were designed to uphold.

Art has played a similarly crucial role in feminist resistance. Throughout history, visual and performance art have been used to challenge gender roles, confront institutionalized sexism, and make oppression visible in ways that words alone often cannot. The feminist art movement of the 1970s was a direct response to the exclusion of women from the mainstream art world, but it was also a challenge to the ways in which women's bodies and experiences had been depicted in male-dominated culture.

Artists like Ana Mendieta used their bodies as part of their work, forcing audiences to confront issues of gender, violence, and erasure. The Guerrilla Girls used street art and anonymous activism to call out sexism in the art world, exposing statistics that revealed the vast disparities in representation between male and female artists. These tactics worked because they could not be ignored. A protest outside of a museum could be dismissed as an isolated event, but posters plastered across the city listing the names of male artists whose works dominated the galleries forced the art world to answer questions it had long avoided.

Modern feminist artists continue this legacy, using digital spaces, public installations, and viral media to bring attention to issues that patriarchal institutions try to suppress. Protest art, whether in the form of street murals, performance pieces, or online campaigns, disrupts public spaces in ways that demand engagement. It is easy for politicians to ignore a petition; it is much harder for them to ignore a 30-foot mural exposing their hypocrisy. It is easy for a corporation to release a generic statement about women's rights; it is much harder for them to maintain credibility when feminist artists take their advertisements and rework them to reveal the exploitation behind their branding. The power of creative activism lies in its ability to shift the battleground, making it impossible for oppressive systems to engage without exposing their own weaknesses.

Social media has amplified the effectiveness of these tactics, allowing feminist movements to mobilize quickly and reach global audiences in ways that were not possible before. Hashtag activism has been one of the most visible forms of digital resistance, with movements like #MeToo and #TimesUp demonstrating how a simple phrase can spark a worldwide conversation.

But beyond hashtags, social media has also enabled entirely new forms of resistance, viral challenges that bring attention to issues in unexpected ways, parody accounts that mock misogynistic figures into irrelevance, coordinated digital campaigns that flood the comment sections of corporations and politicians until they are forced to respond. These tactics work because they take advantage of the very systems that power once used to control narratives. Patriarchy built mainstream media to shape public perception in its favor, but digital activists have turned these platforms into spaces where that control is constantly slipping.

The element of surprise is what makes these tactics so effective. When power expects direct confrontation, it prepares itself accordingly. But when power is confronted in ways it did not anticipate, through humor, through art, through language that rewrites the rules, it loses its ability to dictate the terms of engagement. This is why feminist creativity is not just an accessory to activism; it is activism itself. It is a form of resistance that operates on a different plane, one that cannot be easily absorbed, dismissed, or countered. It does not simply challenge oppression; it makes oppression untenable. And once oppression becomes something that can no longer sustain itself, once its arguments are laughed at instead of debated, once its legitimacy is dismantled not through force but through the simple act of refusing to take it seriously, its fall becomes inevitable.

This is the power of creative resistance. It is not about asking for change; it is about making the status quo impossible to maintain. It is about ensuring that patriarchal systems can no longer operate as they once did, that their language, their narratives, their illusions of power are stripped away piece by piece until there is nothing left to sustain them. The future of resistance does not lie in playing by the rules set by the oppressors; it lies in rewriting the entire game. And once that happens, the system will no longer have a foundation to stand on. It will not be defeated by force, it will collapse under the weight of its own irrelevance.

6
Winning Without Fighting

Winning without fighting is an art that has been perfected by those who understand that power is not always about force but about influence, perception, and strategic positioning. In patriarchal societies, women have historically been denied access to traditional sources of power, political office, economic control, military leadership, but this has never meant they were powerless. Instead, women have had to cultivate influence in ways that were often invisible but no less impactful, mastering the ability to shift perspectives, shape decisions, and move entire institutions without direct confrontation.

The ability to win without fighting is not about passivity or submission; it is about understanding the mechanisms that shape power and using them to alter the balance in ways that make resistance unnecessary. It is about positioning oneself in such a way that change becomes inevitable, not through brute force, but through the gradual, deliberate, and often unnoticed redirection of social, political, and cultural currents.

Soft power has always been one of the most effective tools for social change. Unlike hard power, which relies on coercion, soft power operates through persuasion, trust, and the ability to make people want to align with a particular vision of the world. It is the power of ideas, of cultural influence, of shaping the narratives that determine what is seen as possible, desirable, and legitimate. Women have long been forced to develop this skill out of necessity, influencing outcomes through indirect means because direct confrontation was either impossible or too dangerous. In households, in workplaces, in political movements, women have used persuasion to shift decisions, to build coalitions, and to create the conditions under which their goals could be achieved without the need for direct conflict. This is not a lesser form of power, it is one of the most enduring, and it is one that patriarchal institutions have consistently underestimated.

One of the most powerful aspects of soft power is its ability to shift perceptions in ways that do not immediately provoke resistance. Hard power demands immediate submission, which often leads to backlash and counter-resistance. Soft power, on the other hand, works by aligning people's own self-interests with the goals of the movement, making it easier for them to accept change because they believe it benefits them. This is why some of the most effective social movements have been those that framed their demands not as radical overhauls but as natural progressions.

The fight for women's suffrage, for example, was not won purely through protests and legal battles; it was won by persuading men in power that women's participation in democracy was inevitable, that refusing them the vote was not only unjust but also politically unsustainable. The civil rights movement did not just demand change; it strategically leveraged cultural influence, music, literature, religious rhetoric, to make the moral case for racial justice in ways that appealed to the existing values of those who might otherwise have resisted.

Women today can use these same principles in every sphere of life, from politics to the workplace to community organizing. One of the most effective strategies is to identify the self-interest of those in power and frame feminist goals in ways that align with those interests. This does not mean compromising on principles or diluting the message; it means understanding how to communicate in ways that make resistance less likely.

In the corporate world, for example, diversity and inclusion initiatives have often been more successful when they have been framed not just as ethical imperatives but as business advantages, showing that companies with more women in leadership perform better financially, that workplaces with equitable policies have higher employee retention, that gender balance leads to stronger decision-making. While the moral case for equality should be enough, the reality is that systems built on profit and efficiency respond more quickly when they see equality as beneficial to their bottom line.

Similarly, in politics, shifting policy often requires more than just presenting facts or making demands; it requires understanding the motivations of those in power and using those motivations to advance feminist goals. Policymakers are often more influenced by public pressure, media narratives, and economic interests than by ideological consistency. This means that rather than engaging in direct conflict with those who oppose gender equality, a more effective approach can be to shape the environment in such a way that supporting feminist policies becomes the politically advantageous choice.

This can be done by mobilizing public opinion, by ensuring that gender equity is framed as a mainstream rather than a fringe issue, by making it clear that opposing feminist progress carries social and electoral costs. Politicians do not respond to morality alone, they respond to power. And power, in this context, comes not from fighting head-on but from ensuring that opposition to equality is no longer a viable stance.

The same principles apply in interpersonal and workplace negotiations. One of the most common mistakes women are taught is that power is only achieved through direct assertion, that to get what they want, they must adopt the same aggressive tactics that men use. While assertiveness is important, research consistently shows that women who negotiate in traditionally masculine ways, demanding, positioning themselves as dominant, refusing to compromise, often face backlash in male-dominated spaces. This is not fair, but it is a reality that must be strategically navigated. The most effective negotiators are those who understand that influence is about more than just making demands; it is about making it easy for the other party to say yes. This means framing requests in ways that highlight mutual benefit, using strategic timing, leveraging relationships, and ensuring that proposals are framed as solutions rather than challenges.

In leadership, the most effective women are often those who master the ability to persuade rather than command. While male leaders are often rewarded for displays of dominance, women in leadership are more successful when they use collaboration, relationship-building, and emotional intelligence to drive change. This does not mean that women must always be accommodating or avoid conflict, it means understanding that influence is often more effective than force, that people are more likely to follow leaders who make them feel valued and included than those who simply impose authority.

Studies on leadership have consistently shown that the most enduringly successful leaders, regardless of gender, are those who know how to create buy-in, how to make others feel like they are part of the vision rather than just subjects to it. This is why women who lead with a combination of confidence and strategic empathy are often able to achieve more lasting change than those who rely solely on traditional displays of power.

One of the most overlooked yet powerful aspects of soft power is cultural influence. Laws and policies are important, but the real battle for gender equality is often fought in the realm of culture, what people see as normal, what they believe is possible, what they aspire to. This is why representation matters, why the media, entertainment, and education systems are so crucial in shaping long-term change. The feminist movement has already made enormous strides in this area, shifting cultural expectations about what women can do, what roles they can play, and how they are perceived. But the fight is far from over. There are still deeply ingrained narratives that reinforce gender inequality, that keep women from fully stepping into power, that make misogyny seem like an acceptable, even inevitable, part of society. Winning without fighting means continuing to shape these narratives in ways that make resistance to gender equality not just morally indefensible, but socially and culturally unthinkable.

Soft power does not mean avoiding confrontation or settling for slow progress. It means understanding that change does not always have to be won through battle, it can be won by shifting the ground so completely that the battle is no longer necessary. It is about knowing when to fight and when to let influence do the work. It is about recognizing that the most effective revolutions are often the ones that do not announce themselves as revolutions, that reshape the world so gradually yet so thoroughly that by the time the change is fully realized, it feels inevitable.

Patriarchy has survived for centuries not just through force but through perception, through the illusion that its structures are natural and unchangeable. The key to dismantling it is not just to fight against it, but to ensure that its very foundations are eroded by the weight of new ideas, new expectations, and new forms of power that cannot be easily countered. And that is how women win, not by engaging on the terms of those who oppose them, but by making those terms irrelevant.

Winning without fighting is not about avoiding conflict, it is about understanding that the most effective battles are often won before they are ever fought. The most successful movements, leaders, and strategists throughout history have understood that brute force alone is rarely the most efficient path to victory. Instead, they have relied on persuasion, cultural influence, and psychological positioning to shift the balance of power in their favor. For women seeking to dismantle patriarchal structures, this is a crucial lesson: power is not always about direct confrontation, and in many cases, real transformation happens when those in power are made to believe that change is in their own best interest. This is the essence of soft power, not forcing a change through external pressure alone, but ensuring that resistance to change becomes impractical, unappealing, or even impossible.

One of the greatest advantages of soft power is that it allows movements to operate in ways that are difficult to counter. When demands for change are framed as a direct challenge to authority, those in power have a clear opponent to fight against. They can frame the movement as radical, dangerous, unreasonable. They can use institutional mechanisms to block change, spin public narratives against it, or simply refuse to engage. But when change is introduced through persuasion, through cultural influence, through the gradual redefinition of what is seen as normal and acceptable, opposition becomes much harder to maintain.

This is why some of the most successful feminist victories have not come through direct clashes with patriarchal systems, but through strategic shifts in public perception that have made gender equality seem not just desirable, but inevitable.

A key component of this strategy is the ability to make those in power believe they have something to gain from change. Throughout history, systems of oppression have relied on the idea that those at the top must maintain control at all costs. But what happens when they begin to believe that clinging to the old ways is actually more costly than embracing progress? This is where influence and persuasion become powerful tools.

Women seeking to shift workplace policies, for example, have often found that arguments based solely on fairness or morality are less effective than those that emphasize efficiency, profit, or stability. A CEO may not be moved by the ethical argument for equal pay, but they might reconsider when presented with

84

data showing that gender-diverse leadership teams outperform homogenous ones. A politician may resist calls for paid maternity leave if framed as a social justice issue, but they may be more receptive when shown that economies with strong parental leave policies have higher workforce participation and lower poverty rates.

This approach is not about manipulation, it is about understanding human motivation and using it to create conditions where opposition to change becomes untenable. Resistance to gender equality does not always stem from outright hostility; in many cases, it is rooted in inertia, in the reluctance to disrupt the familiar, in the fear of losing control. But people are far less likely to resist when they see the change as benefiting them, when they believe they have had a role in shaping it, when they do not feel forced into submission but rather led into alignment with a vision that serves their own interests. This is why the most effective feminist movements have not only demanded change but have also created incentives for those in power to adopt it, whether through economic pressure, public opinion, or the slow but steady erosion of outdated cultural norms.

One of the most overlooked aspects of soft power is the ability to change narratives without directly engaging in battle. Traditional activism often focuses on fighting against oppressive ideas, refuting them, proving them wrong. But sometimes, the most effective way to dismantle a harmful narrative is not to argue against it, but to replace it with a more compelling one. This is why storytelling has always been such a critical tool for social change. People do not just respond to facts and logic, hey respond to stories, to emotions, to the sense of possibility that comes with seeing a different world reflected in the narratives around them.

This is why representation in media, literature, and history is so powerful. When women see themselves in leadership roles, in positions of influence, in stories of strength and success, it reshapes what they believe is possible. And just as importantly, when men grow up seeing women in positions of power, they are less likely to resist the idea of gender equality because it no longer feels like a threat, it feels normal.

Cultural influence is often the first step in creating political and institutional change because it shifts what people are willing to accept. Before any major civil rights victory, there was always a period in which the cultural groundwork had to be laid, where artists, writers, filmmakers, and thought leaders had to introduce new ways of thinking that made the old ways seem outdated. Feminism has followed this same pattern. The initial fight for reproductive rights, for example, was not just won in courtrooms, it was won in conversations, in changing attitudes, in making the idea of women's bodily autonomy so widely accepted that laws restricting it began to feel increasingly unjustified.

The same has been true for movements against workplace discrimination, for the dismantling of gender roles in parenting, for the redefinition of masculinity itself. None of these changes happened overnight, and none of them happened solely through confrontation. They happened because feminists understood that before laws could be rewritten, minds had to be changed.

One of the most effective ways to leverage soft power is through coalition-building, bringing together diverse groups of people who may not fully align on every issue but who share enough common ground to push for change together. Patriarchy has survived for centuries in part because it has been able to keep its opposition divided, convincing different groups that their struggles are separate, that they must compete for limited resources and attention. But history has shown that the greatest threats to oppressive systems come when those who have been marginalized find ways to unite. This is why feminist movements have been strongest when they have recognized the intersections of gender with race, class, and other systems of oppression, when they have built alliances with labor movements, civil rights movements, and environmental justice movements. Power is rarely held by a single entity, it is distributed across institutions, across cultural narratives, across the systems that shape daily life. Winning without fighting means recognizing that by shifting power in one area, it is possible to shift it in others as well.

Another critical aspect of soft power is strategic patience, the ability to see beyond the immediate battle and focus on the long-term goal. Oppressive systems thrive on exhaustion, on forcing activists into a constant state of reaction, on making every victory feel temporary and every setback feel permanent. But those who wield soft power effectively understand that real change is not always about immediate wins, it is about setting the stage for inevitable transformation. This means knowing when to push and when to wait, when to apply pressure and when to step back, when to let ideas spread quietly and when to make them loud. It means recognizing that change does not always come in the form of sweeping revolutions, but often in the slow, steady erosion of old norms until they collapse under their own weight.

Winning without fighting is not about complacency, it is about strategy. It is about recognizing that while direct confrontation is sometimes necessary, the most enduring victories are often those that are achieved not through force but through influence. It is about understanding that power is not just about who holds the highest office or the most money, but about who shapes the narratives, who decides what is considered possible, who determines the terms of engagement. It is about making it so that the world moves in a direction where resistance to gender equality is not just ineffective, but unimaginable.

And once that shift happens, once the cultural, political, and social landscape has been reshaped so thoroughly that the fight no longer needs to be fought, the victory is not just won. It is secured.

Winning without fighting is not about surrender or passivity; it is about understanding how to use influence to change the world on a fundamental level. Patriarchy has lasted as long as it has not because it is unassailable, but because it has convinced people, especially women, that it is inevitable. It has embedded itself so deeply in political, economic, and social structures that it appears immovable, something too deeply ingrained to ever be dismantled.

But history shows otherwise. Every oppressive system that once seemed permanent, monarchies ruling by divine right, segregation justified by pseudo-science, legal prohibitions against women's basic freedoms, has eventually crumbled, not just because people fought against them, but because they lost the legitimacy required to sustain them. Influence, persuasion, and cultural shifts have always played a role in these collapses, making it clear that the fight for equality does not always need to be waged through direct confrontation. Sometimes, the most effective way to win is by ensuring that the opposition's position becomes untenable, outdated, and, ultimately, irrelevant.

Understanding soft power requires understanding how people make decisions, how they internalize ideas, how they justify beliefs, and how they adapt when the world around them changes. People do not wake up one day and decide that oppression is wrong; they shift their views gradually, often without realizing it. The role of feminist strategy is to accelerate this process, to introduce new ways of thinking that make patriarchal systems feel not just wrong but impractical. Consider the rapid shift in public perception around marriage equality. For decades, LGBTQ+ activists fought legal battles, organized protests, and made demands. But much of the actual change in attitudes came not from courtrooms but from television shows, books, and real-life visibility. The moment same-sex relationships became a normal, everyday part of public consciousness, resistance to marriage equality began to feel less like a moral stance and more like an outdated relic of another era. The same strategy has been used in gender equality movements, once women in leadership roles became common enough, the idea that they were unfit for power no longer required direct challenge; it simply stopped making sense.

This is why representation matters. Women in positions of power do not just hold those positions for themselves, they shift public perception of what is possible. The more people see women as CEOs, political leaders, military strategists, and innovators, the harder it becomes for patriarchy to justify keeping them out of those spaces. This is not just about individual success; it is about collective transformation. It is about making the exclusion of women from power no longer seem like a rational argument but a sign of regression. Feminist movements have always understood this, which is why they have fought not just for legal rights but for cultural visibility. The goal is not simply to demand a seat at the table but to make it absurd that women were ever excluded in the first place.

Winning without fighting also requires an understanding of leverage, knowing where to apply pressure, when to wait, and when to make a decisive move. Systems of power are not monolithic; they have weaknesses, divisions, and points of vulnerability. The most successful movements exploit these weaknesses, using them to shift power in ways that do not require direct conflict. Consider the way that financial pressure has been used as a tool for feminist change. When companies have refused to implement gender-equitable policies, activists have not always needed to engage in long legal battles; they have simply needed to expose those policies to public scrutiny, leading to consumer boycotts, investor withdrawals, and brand damage. In many cases, businesses have implemented feminist policies not because they had a moral awakening, but because the cost of maintaining the status quo became too high. This is influence at work, not forcing change through direct confrontation, but making it the most logical choice for those in power.

One of the most effective forms of soft power is the ability to set the terms of debate. Patriarchy has survived in part because it has controlled the language of discourse, framing feminist demands as radical, unreasonable, or even dangerous. But when feminist movements take control of the narrative, they make it impossible for patriarchy to sustain itself without constant justification. This is why shifting public opinion is so crucial. It is not enough to present feminist ideas as valid; they must be presented as inevitable. The conversation must move from *should women have equal power?* to *why was this ever a question?* The most successful political and social movements have always operated this way, redefining what is seen as common sense so thoroughly that the opposition is no longer taken seriously.

This is also where humor and satire play a crucial role. Patriarchy relies on maintaining an aura of legitimacy, presenting itself as the natural order of things. But nothing undermines legitimacy faster than ridicule. When feminist movements mock outdated gender roles, when they turn misogynistic arguments into jokes, they strip patriarchy of the serious consideration it needs to sustain itself. A sexist politician who is met not with outrage but with laughter loses credibility. A company that releases a tone-deaf campaign about women's empowerment while exploiting its female workforce is quickly called out, not with outrage alone but with sharp, cutting humor that spreads faster than any official statement could counteract. These are not minor cultural shifts, they are strategic, deliberate ways of eroding the foundations of an oppressive system without engaging it on its own terms.

Another key aspect of winning without fighting is coalition-building. Patriarchy has historically maintained control by dividing its opposition, pitting different marginalized groups against one another, convincing them that their struggles are separate. But power shifts when coalitions form, when women's movements align with labor movements, when gender justice intersects with racial justice, when economic inequality is linked to the fight against misogyny. The feminist movement has at times struggled with this, often sidelining women of color, working-class women, and LGBTQ+ activists in pursuit of a narrow vision of gender equality that centered white, affluent women.

But true feminist power comes from broadening the coalition, from recognizing that patriarchy is not just about gender but about maintaining hierarchies that affect multiple groups in different ways. When these groups recognize their shared interests, the movement becomes unstoppable, not because it fights harder, but because it refuses to be divided.

Winning without fighting also means knowing when to step back and allow patriarchal systems to collapse under their own contradictions. Many of the most oppressive institutions in history have not fallen because of direct attack but because they became unsustainable. Slavery in the U.S. was not just morally indefensible; it became economically unviable. Apartheid in South Africa did not just face moral condemnation; it was increasingly difficult to maintain in the face of global economic and political pressure. Many of the patriarchal structures that still exist today are equally fragile, reliant on outdated models of power that no longer align with the realities of the modern world. Feminist movements do not always need to destroy these structures directly, they often need only to accelerate the conditions under which they collapse on their own.

The ultimate goal of soft power is not just to change laws or policies, but to change the very way people think. To make gender inequality not just illegal but unthinkable. To ensure that the next generation does not have to fight the same battles because the world they inherit has already been reshaped. Winning without fighting is about shifting the foundations so thoroughly that the fight itself becomes unnecessary, because the world has already moved on.

The beauty of this strategy is that it does not require permission. It does not ask those in power to grant women their rights. It does not wait for institutions to decide to change. It moves forward regardless, creating new realities in which patriarchy is no longer sustainable. And when those in power realize that they are no longer in control of the cultural, political, and social direction of the world, they do not need to be fought. They will simply find that they have already lost.

7
Resilience in Battle

Resisting oppression is exhausting. It is designed to be. Patriarchal systems, like all systems of domination, do not just rely on brute force to maintain control, they rely on exhaustion, on attrition, on making the fight so long, so grinding, so relentless that those who resist it eventually give up. The goal is not necessarily to win outright but to outlast the opposition, to wear down those who dare to fight back until they no longer have the strength to continue. This is why one of the most crucial aspects of any long-term struggle for justice is resilience, not just the ability to fight, but the ability to keep fighting. Resilience is not just about physical endurance but about emotional and mental stamina, about finding ways to sustain resistance in the face of setbacks, disappointments, and seemingly endless cycles of backlash.

One of the most effective tools of oppression is the illusion of inevitability. Patriarchy does not just tell women that they are inferior; it tells them that their oppression is permanent, that no amount of effort will change the fundamental structure of the world. This is not just a lie, it is a strategy. The most dangerous thing to any oppressive system is hope, the belief that change is possible, that resistance is not futile, that history is not a fixed narrative but something that can be rewritten. This is why every major feminist victory has been followed by attempts to roll back progress, to remind women that their gains are temporary, that power will always ultimately revert to those who have held it for centuries. It is a psychological war as much as a political one, designed to make women doubt their own agency, to see every setback as proof that their efforts are meaningless rather than as a temporary obstacle in a much longer fight.

Resilience, then, begins with rejecting this narrative of inevitability. It requires understanding that backlash is not a sign of failure but of success. Power does not push back against movements that are ineffective; it pushes back against movements that pose a real threat. Every time women's rights are challenged, every time gains are threatened, it is evidence that those gains were significant enough to cause panic in the institutions that uphold patriarchy. The goal of this backlash is to make women feel like they are losing when, in reality, they are forcing change at a pace that the system can barely keep up with. Recognizing this is crucial because it allows activists and feminists to reframe their struggles, to see challenges not as proof of failure but as confirmation that they are on the right path.

But even with this understanding, the emotional toll of long-term activism is real. The fight for gender equality is not new, and it will not be won overnight. The women who fought for the right to vote, for access to education, for reproductive rights, for workplace protections, for freedom from violence, many of them did not live to see the full results of their efforts. And yet, they fought anyway. They understood something that every activist today must remember: movements are marathons, not sprints. Burnout happens when people expect immediate results, when they believe that one election, one policy, one cultural shift will be enough to permanently dismantle centuries of oppression.

But real change is cumulative, built on decades, sometimes centuries, of effort. It is essential, then, for those engaged in the fight to develop strategies for long-term sustainability, to recognize that self-preservation is not just an individual concern but a political necessity.

One of the biggest myths about activism is that self-care is indulgent, that it is a distraction from the real work of dismantling oppressive systems. But this is a dangerous misconception, one that serves the interests of patriarchy rather than those who seek to challenge it. The reality is that exhaustion and burnout are not just personal struggles; they are systemic issues that weaken movements, that make it easier for oppression to persist. If women are too drained, too demoralized, too broken down by the constant struggle, they are less able to fight effectively. This is why self-care is not a luxury, it is a revolutionary act. It is a way of ensuring that resistance does not just exist in the moment, but that it is sustained for as long as it takes to achieve real transformation.

But self-care does not mean individualism. The capitalist version of self-care, the idea that resilience is about spa days and retail therapy, about taking time for oneself in isolation, is not enough. True resilience comes from community, from collective care, from building networks of support that ensure that no one is left to fight alone. The most effective movements in history have not been those built on individual heroism, but those that understood the necessity of solidarity.

The Black civil rights movement did not survive because of individual leaders alone, it survived because of community networks, because of churches and neighborhood organizations, because of mutual aid. The labor movements that secured workplace protections for millions did not succeed because of a handful of charismatic figures, they succeeded because workers stood together, because they understood that collective power was the only real power. Feminism must operate in the same way. No woman can take on the full weight of dismantling patriarchy alone. The fight must be shared, and support must be structured in ways that prevent burnout before it happens.

This means recognizing the warning signs of fatigue, not just in oneself but in others. Activists must learn to step back when needed, to rest without guilt, to allow others to take the lead when exhaustion sets in. This is not weakness; it is strategy. A movement that relies too heavily on a handful of individuals will always be vulnerable, always at risk of collapse when those individuals burn out or are targeted by the system. True resilience means ensuring that leadership is distributed, that knowledge and skills are shared, that no one person becomes indispensable. This is what makes movements lasting rather than fleeting, it is not just about fighting the fight but about ensuring that the fight can continue no matter what.

Resilience also requires finding sources of hope, of inspiration, of reminders that progress is not just possible but inevitable. History is filled with examples of feminist victories, of moments when the impossible became reality. Women in the 19th century were told they would never have the right to vote. Women in the early 20th century were told they would never be able to control their own reproductive choices. Women in the 1950s were told they would never have careers outside of the home.

In every generation, there have been those who claimed that feminism had gone too far, that women's demands were unreasonable, that equality had already been achieved. And in every generation, those voices have been proven wrong. This is why understanding history is essential to resilience, it provides perspective, it shows that progress is real, that setbacks are temporary, that every battle fought is part of a much larger arc toward justice.

But perhaps the most important aspect of resilience is joy. Oppression is designed to make resistance feel miserable, to ensure that the fight for justice is as draining and demoralizing as possible. This is why joy is itself a form of resistance. Finding joy in community, in creativity, in laughter, in moments of rest, these are not just personal acts; they are acts of defiance. A movement that sustains itself through joy is a movement that cannot be broken. This does not mean ignoring injustice or pretending that the fight is easy. It means recognizing that movements do not survive on anger alone. They survive on love, on connection, on the knowledge that the future being fought for is not just one of survival, but of thriving.

Resilience in battle is not about never feeling tired, never feeling frustrated, never wanting to give up. It is about knowing that those feelings are part of the fight, that they are expected, that they do not mean defeat. It is about knowing when to rest, when to ask for help, when to step back so that others can step forward. It is about understanding that the fight for justice is long, but that it is worth it. Because every step taken, every battle fought, every act of resistance brings the world closer to something better. And as long as that remains true, the fight will continue. Not because it is easy, not because it is fair, but because it is necessary. And because those who resist oppression have always known one thing to be true, resilience is not just survival. It is the refusal to accept anything less than victory.

Resilience is not simply about enduring hardship; it is about finding ways to push forward even when the path ahead feels impossible. The battle against patriarchy, like all struggles against entrenched power, is not a fight that can be won in a single generation. This is what makes the work so difficult, knowing that no matter how much progress is made, there will always be forces trying to pull it back, to undo the victories won, to return the world to a time when the status quo remained unchallenged. This is why movements for justice must not only fight for change but also fight for their own survival.

The greatest threat to feminist progress is not just opposition from those in power; it is exhaustion, disillusionment, the feeling that no matter how much is done, it will never be enough. This is the emotional weight that every activist, every feminist, every person who refuses to accept oppression must learn to carry. And learning to carry it requires more than just willpower, it requires strategy, support, and the ability to sustain the fight for the long haul.

One of the hardest realities of activism is that success is never guaranteed. Many of the most important feminist struggles have been met with fierce resistance, with laws reversed, with policies undone, with cultural shifts fought at every turn. Reproductive rights are rolled back after decades of legal precedent. Hard-won protections in the workplace are eroded by conservative backlash. Sexual harassment cases that seemed to mark a turning point instead result in abusers finding new ways to maintain their power. These moments can be demoralizing, not just because of the tangible setbacks but because they challenge the belief that progress is linear. They make it easy to wonder:

What is the point? Why keep fighting when every victory seems to come with an equally strong wave of opposition? This is where resilience becomes essential, not as an abstract concept, but as a practical tool for survival. Because the truth is, justice is not a straight path. It is not a single battle with a clear beginning and end. It is a war of endurance, one that requires the ability to withstand setbacks without surrendering to despair.

Burnout is not just an individual experience, it is a collective issue that weakens entire movements. Patriarchy and other systems of oppression are structured in ways that deliberately drain those who resist them. This is why feminists and activists often find themselves overwhelmed, not just by the enormity of the work that needs to be done but by the sheer emotional labor required to fight back. The exhaustion does not just come from the battles themselves, but from the endless cycles of having to justify the fight, having to explain why misogyny still exists, having to educate those who refuse to see what is right in front of them.

It is the weight of being told, again and again, that the fight is unnecessary, that things are not as bad as they seem, that equality has already been achieved, that feminists are overreacting. It is the frustration of watching the same arguments be made, the same debates be had, the same lies about gender and power be repeated despite overwhelming evidence to the contrary. It is the exhaustion of knowing that for every step forward, there will always be forces trying to push things backward.

This is why resilience is not just about fighting harder, it is about fighting smarter. It is about recognizing when to step back, when to rest, when to focus energy on battles that can be won rather than wasting strength on those designed to be unwinnable. It is about understanding that not every person can be convinced, that not every argument must be fought, that some people are invested in maintaining oppression and that spending emotional labor trying to change their minds is energy better spent elsewhere. It is about knowing that the goal is not to win every fight in the moment, but to build momentum over time, to create a world where the fight is no longer necessary because the structures of oppression have been so thoroughly dismantled that they can no longer sustain themselves.

One of the most important tools for resilience is community. No one can fight alone. The most effective movements in history have been those that understood the necessity of collective care, movements where activists took care of one another, where burnout was not seen as a personal failing but as a structural issue that required intentional support. This means building networks of solidarity, spaces where exhaustion can be acknowledged, where rest is not seen as weakness but as part of the strategy.

It means ensuring that feminist movements do not just demand justice but also create environments where those fighting for justice can sustain themselves. It means recognizing that activism cannot be about constant urgency, that movements must have cycles of action and reflection, that there must be room for joy, for laughter, for moments of reprieve. Because without those things, the fight becomes too heavy to carry.

The history of feminist struggle is filled with examples of burnout, of movements that fractured under the weight of their own demands, of activists who gave everything they had only to find themselves too drained to continue. Learning from this history means creating structures that prevent that from happening again. It means recognizing that movements cannot rely on a few key leaders, that knowledge and responsibility must be shared, that no one person should bear the full weight of progress alone. It means rejecting the idea that self-sacrifice is the only way to create change, that suffering is proof of dedication. Because movements that require people to destroy themselves in order to achieve justice are movements that will not last.

Self-care, then, must be seen as a revolutionary act, not as an individual indulgence but as a necessary part of movement-building. It is not about stepping away from the fight, it is about ensuring that the fight can continue. It is about making sure that those who resist oppression are not just surviving but thriving, that they have the energy, the mental clarity, and the emotional strength to keep going. It means setting boundaries, recognizing personal limits, and refusing to allow activism to become a cycle of depletion. It means understanding that movements do not just need fighters; they need thinkers, they need strategists, they need people who can sustain the vision even when the immediate results are not visible.

Another crucial component of resilience is hope. Oppressive systems thrive on despair. They want people to believe that change is impossible, that progress is an illusion, that fighting back is pointless. But history tells a different story. Every feminist victory, every shift in social consciousness, every gain

100

in rights and representation was once thought impossible. Women were told they would never be able to vote. They were told they would never have access to higher education. They were told they would never be able to own property, control their own finances, make decisions about their own bodies.

And yet, every one of these things changed, not easily, not without struggle, but because people refused to accept the idea that the world could not be different. This is what must be remembered in moments of despair: that no matter how strong the opposition, no matter how exhausting the fight, history is on the side of those who push forward. The world has never been changed by those who accept it as it is, it has been changed by those who demand something better.

Resilience is not about denying fatigue. It is not about pretending that the fight is easy. It is about knowing that exhaustion is part of the process but not the end of the story. It is about finding ways to continue, even when everything feels impossible. It is about knowing when to rest, when to step back, when to let others carry the weight for a while. It is about building movements that are sustainable, that do not just burn bright and then fade, but that endure, that grow, that evolve over time. Because in the end, resilience is what determines whether a movement succeeds. Not just the strength to fight, but the strength to keep fighting, to keep believing, to keep moving forward even when every force in the world is trying to push back. Because as long as there are people who refuse to give up, the battle is never lost. It is only waiting for the next victory.

Resilience is a quiet, steady kind of strength. It is not the flash of anger that ignites a protest, nor the moment of triumph when a battle is won. It is what remains when the adrenaline fades, when the speeches are over, when the headlines move on, and the work of fighting injustice continues. Resilience is what allows movements to outlast the forces that seek to destroy them, to withstand not just the physical and political challenges of resistance but the psychological and emotional weight of fighting for a world that does not yet exist. It is about endurance, about making sure that the people who fight for change are still standing long after their oppressors have exhausted themselves. It is about cultivating the mindset that even if change is slow, even if setbacks come in waves, every act of resistance adds to the cumulative weight that will eventually tip the scales.

Patriarchy, like all systems of control, is built to wear its challengers down. It does not just fight back, it seeks to grind people into submission, to make resistance so exhausting, so endless, so frustrating that even the most committed activists begin to wonder if change is worth the cost. This is why every feminist movement in history has had to deal with burnout, with disillusionment, with the slow erosion of hope as setbacks pile up and victories are undone.

The enemy is not just misogyny or injustice; it is exhaustion itself, the creeping belief that nothing will ever change, that the weight of oppression is simply too great to lift. This is why resilience must be cultivated with as much intention as any other strategy of resistance. It is not an afterthought. It is not a secondary concern. It is one of the most important weapons in the fight for justice because no battle can be won if those fighting it are too drained to continue.

One of the first steps in building resilience is accepting that setbacks are inevitable. This is not a sign of failure; it is part of the process. No movement has ever achieved complete victory in a single generation. The abolition of slavery did not end racial injustice. The right to vote did not end gender inequality. Legalized abortion did not ensure universal reproductive freedom. Every gain made has been followed by backlash, by attempts to roll back progress, by new forms of oppression designed to replace the old ones. This is how power operates, it does not simply surrender when challenged; it adapts, it finds new ways to maintain control, it shifts the battlefield so that the fight must be fought again and again. Understanding this is crucial because it prevents despair from taking root. It allows activists to see the long arc of history, to recognize that even when progress is reversed, the struggle is not lost. It means knowing that just as oppression reinvents itself, so too must resistance.

This is why long-term vision is essential. Feminist movements must think beyond immediate goals, beyond singular victories, beyond individual policy changes. The fight is not just for the next law, the next election, the next court ruling, it is for a cultural transformation so deep that future generations do not have to fight the same battles.

This means shifting the focus from short-term wins to long-term sustainability, from momentary outrage to ongoing mobilization. It means building institutions that will outlast any one movement, organizations that will carry on the work even when individual activists burn out. It means investing in education, in media, in the shaping of public consciousness so that the next wave of feminists does not have to start from scratch but can build on the foundation of those who came before them.

Resilience also requires an understanding of power, how it works, how it shifts, and how it can be undermined. Patriarchy is not an immovable monolith; it is a structure that relies on compliance, on the willingness of people to accept its rules, to internalize its logic, to believe that the world it has created is the only possible reality. This is why one of the most effective forms of resistance is simply refusing to accept those rules.

Women who reject the idea that they must be likable to be heard, who refuse to shrink themselves to make others comfortable, who demand space rather than waiting for it to be given, these acts of defiance, though they may seem small, chip away at the foundations of patriarchal power. Every time a woman refuses to be silenced, every time she refuses to accept less than she deserves, every time she supports another woman instead of competing against her, she is participating in a revolution. And revolutions, when sustained, change everything.

This is why community is essential. No one can fight alone, and no one should have to. The strongest movements are those that recognize the importance of mutual support, that create networks of care to ensure that activists do not burn out, that leaders do not become isolated, that those who fight are not left to struggle in silence. This means fostering relationships that go beyond political work, that provide emotional as well as strategic support, that remind those in the fight that they are not alone. It means recognizing that activism is not just about the struggle, it is also about the relationships built in the process, about the solidarity that makes the work possible. It is about creating spaces where people can rest without guilt, where they can recharge without feeling as though they are abandoning the cause, where they can find joy even in the midst of battle.

Because joy is just as much a part of resilience as strategy. Oppression is designed to make resistance feel miserable, to ensure that those who fight for justice are too exhausted to imagine a better future. This is why joy must be cultivated deliberately, why it must be recognized as a form of defiance. A movement that only operates on anger and frustration will eventually burn out. But a movement that finds ways to celebrate, to uplift, to create moments of happiness even in the darkest times, that is a movement that can survive anything. This is why feminist spaces must be spaces of joy as well as resistance.

It is why art, music, storytelling, and laughter are as much tools of revolution as policy proposals and legal challenges. It is why self-care, when practiced collectively, becomes not just an individual act but a political statement: We refuse to be destroyed by the systems that seek to break us.

Resilience is also about adaptability. Movements that remain rigid, that rely on a single strategy, that refuse to evolve with the changing landscape of oppression, will eventually falter. This is why feminist movements must be dynamic, willing to reassess tactics, willing to shift strategies as needed. It means recognizing that what worked in one era may not work in another, that resistance must be flexible, that the ability to pivot is just as important as the ability to persist. It means not becoming attached to a single way of fighting but instead focusing on the larger goal, understanding that the path to justice is not a straight line but a constantly shifting, constantly evolving journey.

And finally, resilience requires belief, not just in the movement, but in the possibility of victory. This is the hardest thing to hold onto in moments of exhaustion, when the weight of oppression feels too great, when the setbacks seem overwhelming. But belief is what sustains movements through the hardest times. It is what allows people to keep fighting even when change seems distant, even when the odds seem insurmountable. It is what has carried every feminist movement forward, from the suffragists to the labor organizers to the reproductive rights activists to the women who are still fighting today. It is the understanding that no matter how long the fight takes, no matter how many setbacks occur, no matter how many times the world tries to push back, the future belongs to those who refuse to give up.

This is what resilience is. It is not about never feeling tired, never feeling frustrated, never feeling the urge to walk away. It is about choosing, again and again, to keep going anyway. It is about knowing that the fight is long but that it is worth it. It is about understanding that progress is not measured by a single victory but by the collective effort of those who refuse to accept anything less than justice. It is about making sure that no matter how much patriarchy tries to wear people down, the movement remains strong, steady, and unbreakable. Because the greatest weapon against oppression is not just resistance, it is endurance. And as long as women endure, as long as they continue to push forward, the fight is never lost. It is only waiting for the next victory.

8
Adapting to Change

Adapting to change is not just a survival skill, it is a strategy for winning. The world does not stand still, and neither does oppression. The systems that enforce patriarchy are constantly shifting, adjusting to new cultural norms, new technologies, and new political realities. What worked in one era to suppress women's power may not work in the next, so those who benefit from oppression learn to evolve, to disguise their motives, to package old injustices in new language, new policies, new technologies that appear progressive while achieving the same restrictive goals. This is why feminism must be just as adaptable, why those who fight for justice cannot afford to become complacent or wedded to a single way of doing things.

Movements that do not evolve get left behind, allowing those in power to stay ahead, to anticipate and counter every challenge before it has a chance to take root. The key to long-term success is not just resisting change but mastering it, using it, turning it into an advantage rather than a disadvantage. Agility is not a sign of weakness; it is the mark of a movement that intends to win.

One of the greatest challenges facing any movement is the assumption that the strategies that worked in the past will continue to work indefinitely. The feminist movement has seen this firsthand. The battles for legal rights, workplace protections, and reproductive autonomy required one set of strategies, lawsuits, protests, media campaigns, electoral politics, but the challenges of the 21st century require a different kind of thinking. The war on women's rights today does not always come in the form of outright legal bans; it comes in the form of economic coercion, of digital manipulation, of social conditioning that convinces people that feminism is no longer necessary even as inequality remains widespread. It comes in the form of corporate feminism, where companies sell empowerment as a brand while continuing to exploit women workers. It comes in the form of artificial intelligence and digital surveillance, where bias is baked into the very algorithms that shape hiring practices, healthcare, and financial decisions. If feminism does not evolve to meet these new forms of oppression, it risks becoming a relic, a movement that won past battles but failed to anticipate the next ones.

This is why adaptability must be a core feminist value. The ability to recognize shifts in power, to analyze new technologies and cultural movements with a critical eye, to predict how patriarchy will attempt to reassert itself in different forms, these are not just intellectual exercises. They are survival tools. They are what separate movements that make history from those that fade into irrelevance. Consider how quickly the landscape of activism has changed in just a few decades.

In the 1960s and 70s, feminist organizing relied on print media, on consciousness-raising meetings, on physical gatherings where women could strategize in person. By the 1990s and early 2000s, cable news and mainstream media became primary battlegrounds, with feminist voices pushing their way into national conversations through televised debates, opinion pieces, and political advocacy. Now, in the digital age, the fight has shifted once again, social media platforms, online communities, data-driven campaigns, and viral storytelling have become the dominant tools of influence.

Movements that fail to adapt to these changes risk becoming obsolete, outpaced by the very forces they seek to challenge. Feminism must not only participate in these shifts but anticipate them, shaping the future rather than simply reacting to it. This means understanding the power of digital activism while also recognizing its limitations. Social media allows feminist movements to reach millions of people in ways that were never possible before, but it also creates new vulnerabilities, misinformation spreads as quickly as truth, online harassment is weaponized to silence dissent, and algorithms are designed to prioritize engagement over accuracy. Feminists who rely solely on digital activism without building real-world structures of power will find themselves at the mercy of corporate-controlled platforms that can change the rules at any time. This is why adaptability must be holistic, balancing new tools with old wisdom, using technology to amplify organizing efforts rather than replace them.

The ability to pivot in response to changing circumstances is not just a skill for movements; it is a necessity for individuals as well. Women in positions of leadership, whether in politics, business, or activism, must learn to navigate shifting power dynamics without losing sight of their principles. The world is full of examples of women who have successfully reinvented themselves in response to changing realities, using adversity as an opportunity for growth rather than a reason to retreat.

Consider the women who have led political revolutions, adapting their strategies as circumstances changed, figures like Angela Davis, who moved from radical Black liberation struggles to global human rights activism, or Malala Yousafzai, who transitioned from a local education advocate in Pakistan to an international symbol of resistance against gender-based oppression. Their power came not just from their message but from their ability to evolve, to stay relevant, to recognize when old strategies were no longer enough and new approaches were needed.

The same lesson applies in the workplace, where adaptability is often the difference between success and stagnation. Women continue to face unique challenges in professional environments, glass ceilings may have been shattered in some industries, but new barriers have replaced them. The expectation that women must constantly prove themselves, that they must balance competence with likability, that they must navigate sexist office politics while also excelling in their jobs, these pressures have not disappeared, even as more women enter positions of power. The key to surviving and thriving in these environments is understanding that rules are always changing, that success is often less about playing by the existing rules and more about knowing when to rewrite them. Women who succeed in male-dominated fields are often those who learn to read the landscape, who recognize shifts in corporate culture, who anticipate industry trends before they happen. They do not simply demand a seat at the table; they change the way the table is set.

Cultural adaptability is just as crucial as political or professional agility. The feminist movement has struggled with this at times, failing to fully integrate the perspectives of marginalized women, resisting new frameworks that challenge traditional feminist narratives. For feminism to remain relevant, it must be willing to evolve, to listen, to make space for new voices and new ideas. This means recognizing that the experiences of Black women, Indigenous women, queer women, disabled women, and working-class women are not secondary concerns but central to the movement's future. It means embracing intersectionality not just as a buzzword but as a fundamental principle, ensuring that feminism is not just about the concerns of the most privileged women but about dismantling oppression in all its forms.

One of the most powerful examples of adaptability in feminist history comes from the women's labor movement, where workers have repeatedly reinvented their strategies in response to changing economic conditions. In the early 20th century,

110

factory workers organized union strikes, using collective action to demand better wages and working conditions. In the 21st century, women in the gig economy are finding new ways to organize, leveraging digital platforms to expose workplace abuses and demand fair treatment from tech giants like Uber, Amazon, and Google. The fight is the same, but the battlefield has changed, and those who recognize this, who understand that feminism must evolve alongside capitalism, technology, and social structures, are the ones who will carry the movement forward.

Adapting to change does not mean abandoning core values. It means recognizing that principles must be upheld in ways that match the world as it is, not as it was. It means refusing to be locked into outdated tactics that no longer serve the cause. It means being willing to challenge traditional feminist orthodoxies when they no longer reflect the realities of the present. It means embracing new forms of resistance, new alliances, new methods of organizing, and new ways of thinking about power.

The ability to stay agile and relevant is what will determine the success of feminist movements in the years to come. The world is changing at a pace faster than ever before, and those who refuse to adapt will find themselves left behind. The question is not whether feminism can survive in this new era, it is whether it will lead the charge into the future or be dragged along by it. The answer depends on the ability to recognize shifts in power, to anticipate new challenges before they arise, and to turn moments of crisis into opportunities for reinvention. Because in the end, adaptability is not just about survival. It is about victory.

Adaptability is a skill that feminist movements and individuals must master to remain effective in an ever-changing world. Power structures do not remain static, nor do the methods of oppression they rely upon. Those who benefit from patriarchy are constantly innovating, shifting tactics, and learning from the past to maintain their dominance. What was once achieved through overt discrimination is now enforced through subtler means, through legal loopholes, economic pressure, algorithmic bias, and cultural messaging designed to make oppression appear voluntary rather than imposed. This is why adaptability is not just useful but necessary. The feminist movement cannot afford to be reactive; it must be proactive, anticipating changes before they happen, staying ahead of those who seek to maintain control, and refusing to become trapped in outdated methods that no longer serve the cause. Agility is power, and those who learn to wield it effectively will determine the future of the struggle for gender justice.

One of the biggest threats to any social movement is the temptation to cling too tightly to past successes, to believe that because a particular strategy worked before, it will work forever. The history of feminism offers countless examples of this challenge. The first wave of feminism fought for and won the right to vote, believing that political representation would naturally lead to broader social and economic equality. But as soon as women secured the vote, they found that legal enfranchisement alone did not dismantle the patriarchal structures that still dictated their lives.

The second wave sought to expand feminism beyond legal rights, challenging gender roles, workplace discrimination, and sexual violence. It made significant progress, but in doing so, it often failed to account for the experiences of women of color, working-class women, and LGBTQ+ communities, leading to necessary critiques from the third wave, which emphasized intersectionality and inclusivity. Each wave of feminism had to evolve beyond the limitations of the one before it, recognizing that oppression adapts and that resistance must do the same.

Today, feminism faces new challenges that demand even greater adaptability. One of the most significant is the rise of digital technology and the ways in which it has reshaped the landscape of activism, discourse, and oppression itself. Social media has given feminists an unprecedented ability to organize, to spread information rapidly, and to hold those in power accountable. Hashtags like #MeToo, #TimesUp, and #SayHerName have mobilized millions, forcing long-overdue conversations about gender violence and systemic injustice. But these digital tools are also double-edged swords. The same platforms that amplify feminist voices are also used to silence them through harassment, doxxing, and coordinated disinformation campaigns. The internet has allowed new forms of misogyny to flourish, from incel subcultures and online radicalization to AI-driven biases that reinforce gender disparities in hiring, policing, and finance. The question is not whether feminism should engage in digital activism, it must, but how it can do so while protecting itself from the vulnerabilities that come with relying on corporate-controlled platforms for mobilization.

To remain effective, feminists must develop digital literacy as a core skill. This means understanding how algorithms shape public perception, how misinformation spreads, and how online movements can be co-opted or diluted by those who wish to neutralize their impact. It means building independent platforms that are not beholden to the interests of tech giants, recognizing that companies like Meta, Google, and X (formerly Twitter) ultimately serve profit rather than justice. It means ensuring that feminist activism is not just viral but sustainable, that it moves beyond temporary outrage and into long-term structural change. The lessons of past movements remain relevant here, flashpoint moments are important, but without institutions, without infrastructure, without a clear strategy for turning attention into action, movements risk fizzling out before they achieve lasting impact.

Beyond technology, feminism must also adapt to the shifting political and economic landscapes that shape the realities of women's lives. In many parts of the world, there has been a well-documented backlash against feminism, with far-right movements actively working to roll back gender equality under the guise of "family values" or "tradition." The overturning of Roe v. Wade in the United States was not just an attack on reproductive rights; it was a warning that progress is not permanent, that every gain can be undone if movements do not remain vigilant. Meanwhile, economic systems continue to exploit women in new and insidious ways. The gender pay gap persists, but now it is exacerbated by gig work and informal labor markets that make it harder to demand fair wages. The expectation that women perform unpaid emotional and domestic labor has not disappeared, it has simply been repackaged under the rhetoric of "hustle culture" and "work-life balance." Capitalism has learned to commodify feminist language, selling "empowerment" as a brand while ensuring that actual economic power remains out of reach for most women.

To navigate these challenges, feminism must evolve beyond resistance and into the realm of strategy. Protests and advocacy will always be essential, but they must be paired with the ability to anticipate how patriarchal systems will try to counter them. This means thinking like those in power, studying their methods, understanding their weaknesses, and developing solutions before problems arise. It means recognizing patterns in history and identifying where the next battles will take place before they happen. It means moving away from short-term reactive thinking and embracing a long-term vision that does not just fight against the existing system but builds alternatives to it.

One of the best examples of this kind of strategic adaptation can be seen in women-led organizations that have successfully reinvented themselves in response to changing conditions. Consider the evolution of reproductive justice movements. In the 1970s, the fight for abortion rights focused primarily on legal access to safe procedures. But as anti-abortion forces shifted their tactics, closing clinics, passing restrictive laws, and using economic barriers to prevent access, reproductive justice

114

movements adapted. They expanded their scope beyond abortion to include broader issues of healthcare access, racial disparities in maternal mortality, and economic justice for parents. They recognized that legal rights were meaningless if people could not afford to exercise them. This shift in strategy made the movement more resilient, harder to undermine, and more inclusive of the communities most affected by reproductive oppression.

Another example can be found in labor movements led by women. In the early days of industrialization, women fought for workplace protections through union organizing. Today, as traditional unions decline and labor exploitation shifts into new forms, freelance work, gig economies, corporate surveillance, women are developing new ways to fight back. Organizations like the National Domestic Workers Alliance and the Fight for $15 movement have adapted by focusing on coalition-building, legislative advocacy, and digital organizing. They have recognized that the battle for fair wages and safe working conditions must evolve alongside the economy, that traditional union models may no longer be sufficient, and that power must be built in new ways.

These lessons apply to individual women as well. In a rapidly changing world, adaptability is not just a political necessity but a personal survival skill. The ability to recognize shifts in workplace culture, to navigate evolving social expectations, to anticipate how new technologies will impact job security, safety, and access to resources, these are all crucial competencies. Women who succeed in male-dominated industries often do so not by conforming to outdated models of leadership but by challenging them, by finding new ways to assert power that do not rely on mimicry of traditional, patriarchal norms. The same is true in activism, leaders who remain effective are those who understand when to pivot, when to let go of outdated methods, and when to embrace new approaches.

Ultimately, the ability to stay agile and relevant is what will determine the future of feminist movements. The world will not slow down for feminism to catch up, if anything, the pace of change is accelerating. The question is not whether women's rights will continue to be challenged; they will. The question is whether feminists will be prepared, whether they will have the foresight to see what is coming and the flexibility to respond effectively. The ability to adapt is what has kept feminist movements alive for generations, and it is what will ensure that they continue to thrive. Because feminism is not just about resisting change, it is about shaping it, directing it, and ensuring that the future is one where justice is not just an aspiration, but a reality.

Adapting to change is not just about reacting to shifting circumstances, it is about shaping the future before oppressive systems have a chance to set new terms. Patriarchy, like all forms of systemic control, does not simply disappear when challenged; it mutates, disguising itself in different language, using new tools to maintain old hierarchies. The history of feminism is filled with examples of moments when the movement had to either evolve or risk irrelevance. When women won the right to vote, some feminists believed the fight was over.

When workplace protections were secured in the 1970s, there were voices that suggested gender equality had been achieved. When #MeToo exploded in 2017, there were those who claimed it marked a permanent shift in how society treats women's experiences. But each of these moments, significant as they were, did not represent the end of the fight, only new phases of it. And in each of those phases, feminism had to reassess its strategies, refine its goals, and prepare for the inevitable backlash that comes whenever power is forced to make concessions.

Understanding this cycle is critical to staying ahead of the forces that seek to maintain the status quo. The push for progress always triggers resistance. The moment gains are made, those in power work to undo them, often by repackaging old forms of oppression in ways that appear modern, even progressive. This is why feminists must constantly question not only their opponents but also the narratives they are fed by institutions that claim to be allies. Consider the rise of "corporate feminism," where companies market empowerment while continuing to exploit female labor. They sell T-shirts that say *Girl Boss* while underpaying their female employees. They produce commercials about women's strength while opposing paid maternity leave and workplace protections. They co-opt feminist language not to advance equality but to neutralize it, to turn it into a commodity rather than a call to action.

And this tactic is not unique to corporations, it is used by politicians who claim to support gender equality while passing laws that restrict women's bodily autonomy. It is used by media outlets that celebrate "powerful women" while still enforcing impossible beauty standards and scrutinizing female leaders more harshly than their male counterparts. It is used by patriarchal systems that, instead of outright denying women's rights, create enough superficial progress to convince people that the struggle is over while ensuring that real power remains concentrated in the same hands.

This is why adaptability requires skepticism, not just of obvious enemies, but of supposed victories. Every gain must be examined critically. Every policy that claims to advance gender equality must be assessed not just for what it says but for how it is implemented. Every public figure who claims to support women's rights must be judged by their actions, not just their words. This does not mean rejecting progress, it means refusing to be pacified by symbolic gestures when structural change is still needed. It means recognizing when feminism is being used as a marketing tool rather than a revolutionary force. And it means ensuring that movements are not lulled into complacency by the illusion of change when the reality remains largely the same.

One of the greatest challenges in staying agile is the tendency of movements to become rigid over time. What begins as radical and disruptive can, if not careful, become institutionalized, bureaucratic, and slow to respond to new realities. Many early feminist organizations struggled with this, becoming so focused on maintaining their existing structures that they failed to adapt to the needs of the next generation.

This has been particularly evident in the tension between older feminist activists and younger women who approach gender justice from different perspectives. The feminist concerns of the 1970s, focused on workplace equality, legal protections, and reproductive rights, are not the same as the concerns of younger feminists today, who also grapple with digital harassment, environmental justice, and the intersection of gender with race, class, and sexuality in ways that earlier movements did not always prioritize. The failure to integrate these evolving perspectives has, at times, led to fragmentation within feminism, with different generations feeling alienated from one another rather than working in coalition.

To remain relevant, feminism must be a living, evolving force, one that is willing to challenge its own assumptions, to incorporate new understandings of oppression, and to engage with the changing ways that patriarchy operates. This means being open to new ideas, even when they feel uncomfortable. It means listening to younger activists rather than dismissing them as naive. It means recognizing that new generations will not fight the same way that past generations did, and that this is not a sign of failure but of growth. It means being willing to abandon outdated strategies when they no longer serve the movement, even if they were once effective. And it means resisting the urge to create hierarchies within feminism itself, where some voices are prioritized over others based on arbitrary measures of experience or credibility.

Part of this adaptability also requires an understanding of how external forces will attempt to divide and weaken feminist movements. Patriarchy has always relied on division as a tactic for maintaining control, pitting women against each other, convincing different marginalized groups that their struggles are separate rather than interconnected. This is why feminist movements must be vigilant against internal divisions that are manufactured by those in power.

One of the most effective ways to neutralize a movement is to create infighting, to encourage ideological purity tests that make coalition-building impossible, to turn activists against one another over minor disagreements while the real enemy remains untouched. This does not mean ignoring differences or avoiding difficult conversations, it means approaching them with the awareness that division benefits those who want feminism to fail. It means prioritizing shared goals over individual egos. It means recognizing that the feminist movement is strongest when it is broad, diverse, and inclusive rather than rigidly dogmatic.

Another key component of staying agile is the ability to balance long-term vision with immediate action. Movements that focus only on the future risk losing relevance in the present, while movements that only react to crises risk losing sight of the bigger picture. The most effective feminist organizing happens when both of these perspectives are integrated, when immediate battles are fought within the context of a larger strategy, when short-term victories are used as stepping stones toward systemic change. This requires discipline. It requires resisting the urge to get lost in the constant cycle of outrage that social media encourages, where every new scandal demands an immediate response but few lead to sustained action. It requires knowing when to engage and when to step back, when to fight and when to build. It requires ensuring that feminism is not just about reacting to the latest crisis but about creating the conditions where those crises no longer occur in the first place.

Ultimately, adaptability is what will determine whether feminism continues to be a force for real change or whether it becomes another co-opted movement, absorbed into the institutions it once sought to challenge. The world will not wait for feminism to catch up. Patriarchy will continue to evolve, will continue to find new ways to enforce gender inequality, will continue to test the movement's ability to respond. The only way to stay ahead is to embrace change, to remain flexible, to recognize that resistance must be as dynamic as the systems it opposes. This does not mean abandoning core feminist principles, it means applying them in ways that are suited to the realities of today, not yesterday.

Feminism must be willing to disrupt itself in order to stay relevant. It must be willing to question its own practices, to challenge its own assumptions, to take risks, to experiment with new strategies even when old ones feel comfortable. It must be unafraid to reinvent itself again and again, knowing that the goal is not to preserve a static vision of feminism but to create a world in which feminism is no longer needed. And until that world exists, adaptability will remain one of the most powerful tools in the feminist arsenal. Because those who refuse to change will be left behind, but those who learn to move with the shifting tides of power will shape the future itself.

9
Defining Victory

Victory is not always the grand, cinematic moment of triumph that history books and Hollywood films would have us believe. In the struggle for justice, particularly in the fight against patriarchy, success is rarely delivered in a single sweeping gesture. It does not come with a clear ending, a final battle in which all wrongs are made right, and those who have oppressed others are suddenly defeated and held accountable. That is a fantasy, and like all fantasies, it serves a purpose, offering motivation, providing hope, but it can also be a trap. If we measure victory only in terms of total transformation, we risk failing to see the real, meaningful changes that accumulate over time, the shifts in power that do not happen in a single moment but in thousands of small, strategic moves.

The problem with traditional definitions of victory is that they are often shaped by the very systems we seek to dismantle. The idea that success must be immediate, total, and universally recognized is itself a patriarchal construction, rooted in the myth of the individual hero, the singular leader who wins the battle, claims the throne, and changes the course of history alone. This is not how change happens, and it has never been how women's liberation has been won. Feminist victories have always been collective, incremental, and, more often than not, unglamorous. They have been the slow, steady shifts that take place over years, sometimes decades, of persistent effort. They are the policies rewritten after years of legal battles, the cultural norms eroded by generations of resistance, the ideas that seemed radical in one era but become common sense in the next.

To define victory on one's own terms means rejecting the narrow framework that says success must be immediate or visible to be meaningful. It means recognizing that every feminist action, no matter how small, contributes to a larger movement, and that impact is not always measured in headlines or history books. A woman who negotiates a higher salary for herself has won a victory, not just because she earns more, but because she challenges the expectation that women should accept less. A woman who refuses to stay silent in the face of workplace harassment is victorious, even if the consequences of her speaking out do not immediately result in policy changes, because she sets a precedent for others. A woman who raises a child to question sexism and injustice is reshaping the future, even if that impact is not immediately obvious. These are not minor actions. They are the foundation of systemic change.

One of the biggest obstacles to recognizing these victories is the way patriarchy conditions women to see their successes as insignificant or unworthy of celebration. Women are taught to downplay their accomplishments, to believe that unless they have changed the entire world, their efforts do not count. This is a deliberate tactic of oppression, convincing people that unless they have dismantled the entire system, their work is meaningless ensures that they remain exhausted, disheartened, and ultimately, more likely to give up. But those who hold power understand something that many activists forget: real change happens in accumulation. It happens when enough people push back in enough ways that the system begins to bend, that the center of gravity shifts, that the old ways of doing things become unsustainable.

This is why personal victories matter, not just for the individuals who achieve them, but for the collective movement. Every woman who carves out a space for herself in a male-dominated industry makes it easier for the next woman to do the same. Every woman who asserts her right to autonomy and self-determination weakens the structures that seek to control women's lives. Every conversation that challenges sexist assumptions, every act of solidarity that refuses to pit women against each other, every rejection of patriarchal expectations, these are victories. They may not make the front page of the newspaper, but they make a difference. They are the steps that lead to cultural shifts, the cracks in the foundation of oppression that will eventually cause it to collapse.

Feminist history is full of victories that were not recognized as such in their own time. The women who fought for suffrage did not live to see the full effects of their work. Those who led early labor movements for fair wages and safe working conditions could not have predicted the full extent of the worker protections their efforts would eventually inspire. The activists who challenged sexual harassment in the 1970s and 80s likely could not have imagined a world in which millions would unite under the banner of #MeToo. These victories were not immediate, nor were they the work of any single person. They were cumulative. They were the result of countless women, many of whom were never publicly acknowledged, doing the work without guarantees of success, without the promise of seeing the change they fought for in their lifetimes. But their victories endure because they refused to let the lack of immediate recognition define the value of their efforts.

This is the mindset that must be cultivated now. The fight for gender equality is far from over, and like those who came before, the women fighting today may not see the full results of their work. That does not mean the work is in vain. It means understanding that feminism is not just about winning a single battle, but about shifting the conditions of the world so thoroughly that future generations do not have to fight the same wars. This requires patience, persistence, and a willingness to recognize success in its many forms.

To define victory on one's own terms also means rejecting the idea that feminist success must always align with traditional measures of power. Women have been told that breaking the glass ceiling, becoming CEOs, presidents, billionaires, is the ultimate marker of gender equality. But individual success within patriarchal structures does not necessarily mean those structures have changed. A woman in a position of power who upholds the same policies that harm other women is not a feminist victory. A handful of women achieving wealth while millions remain in poverty is not systemic progress. This is why defining victory must go beyond personal ambition, it must be collective, expansive, and rooted in justice.

Victory must also be understood in terms of survival. For many women, simply existing in defiance of a world that seeks to diminish them is an act of resistance. Surviving abuse, discrimination, or systemic injustice and continuing to fight for oneself and others is a victory. Refusing to internalize the messages that say women are less than, refusing to conform to expectations that demand compliance, refusing to be silent when speaking up carries risk, these are victories, too. And they are just as important as the larger political and legal battles that feminist movements engage in.

In redefining success, it is also important to acknowledge that victories do not always look like victories at first. Sometimes, what seems like failure is actually the groundwork for something bigger. A protest that does not immediately change policy still raises awareness. A lawsuit that is lost can still expose systemic corruption. A cultural shift that seems slow or incomplete is still a shift. The key is not to measure success only by what is achieved in the moment, but by the way each action contributes to a larger trajectory of change.

Defining victory on your own terms means refusing to let external forces dictate what success should look like. It means recognizing that real change is not always immediate or obvious. It means valuing incremental progress, personal acts of resistance, and the collective power of small victories. It means understanding that the feminist movement is not a sprint, but a relay, where each generation builds upon the work of those who came before, ensuring that the fight continues until true justice is achieved. Victory is not a destination. It is a process, a commitment, a refusal to accept anything less than full equality. And as long as that fight continues, every step forward is a win.

Victory is often framed as a singular moment, a final, decisive event that marks the end of struggle and the beginning of a new reality. This is how history is told, with clean beginnings and clear endings, as though the fight for justice follows a straightforward trajectory, with a victory parade waiting at the finish line. But this is not how real change happens. The world does not transform overnight, and power does not concede simply because it is asked to do so. Those who benefit from oppression understand this better than anyone. They are patient.

They plan for the long game, ensuring that even when they lose a battle, they are prepared to reclaim their influence through different means, to repurpose old methods of control in new disguises. This is why feminists must resist the urge to see success only in absolute terms, because doing so allows opponents of progress to manipulate expectations, to convince people that if injustice still exists, then the entire movement has failed.

This is the danger of defining victory too narrowly. If success is measured only in terms of immediate, sweeping change, then setbacks become catastrophic, and exhaustion becomes inevitable. This is how movements are worn down, not just through outright defeat, but through the slow erosion of hope, the sense that no matter how much work is done, it will never be enough. But what if victory is not just the final result, but also the process itself? What if success is measured not only by the laws changed, the policies enacted, or the institutions restructured, but by the people who refuse to be silenced, the ideas that persist despite opposition, the cultural norms that begin to shift even before those in power acknowledge them? What if every act of resistance, no matter how small, is understood as part of a cumulative, long-term victory?

This perspective is necessary because oppression is not static. It adapts, it evolves, it finds ways to reinforce itself even as progress is made. Consider the trajectory of women's rights over the last century. The legal recognition of women as full citizens was a victory. The right to vote was a victory. The ability to access education, the workplace, birth control, legal protections against harassment, each of these was a victory. But none of them ended the fight. Every gain was met with backlash, with attempts to reverse or limit what had been won.

Women gained the right to work outside the home, but wage inequality and workplace discrimination ensured that economic independence remained elusive for many. Women gained reproductive rights, but anti-choice forces continually found ways to restrict access, creating financial, legal, and logistical barriers that turned a supposed right into a privilege available only to some. The lesson is clear: victories must be defended, reinforced, and built upon, because those who fear gender equality are always working to take back what has been won.

This does not mean that victories are meaningless. It means that they are not the end of the story. They are stepping stones, foundations upon which further progress is built. And this is why it is crucial to celebrate them, not just the landmark moments, but the everyday wins that push the movement forward in ways that may not always be visible at first. A woman negotiating a fairer salary for herself may not seem like

126

a historic event, but in doing so, she challenges the expectation that women should accept less. A woman speaking up against sexist policies in her workplace may not single-handedly change corporate culture, but she plants a seed, making space for others to challenge injustice as well. A woman who refuses to internalize patriarchal messaging, who teaches her daughter that her worth is not tied to her appearance, who supports other women instead of competing with them, who refuses to make herself smaller to accommodate fragile male egos, she, too, is reshaping the world, even if her name never appears in a history book.

One of the most insidious tactics of oppression is to make people believe that small actions do not matter. Patriarchy thrives on the illusion that power is an immovable force, that the efforts of individuals are insignificant in the face of larger systems. This is a lie designed to keep people passive. The truth is that power is always vulnerable to disruption, and history is shaped not only by grand revolutions but by the accumulation of countless individual acts of defiance. Every cultural shift that seemed impossible at one point, abolition, civil rights, marriage equality, was achieved not by a single, dramatic event, but by years of relentless pressure, by people who refused to accept that their efforts were meaningless.

Defining victory on one's own terms also means resisting the pressure to conform to traditional measures of success. Women have long been told that their achievements must be validated by external approval, by official recognition, by financial gain or institutional power. But feminism is not about replicating patriarchal models of success; it is about creating new definitions of power, new ways of valuing impact and influence. A woman who chooses to prioritize community over corporate ambition is just as successful as a woman who rises to the top of her profession, if not more so, given that many professional environments remain structured to reward conformity to patriarchal norms rather than real progress. A woman who refuses to compromise her values in exchange for token representation in male-dominated spaces is defining success on her own terms. A woman who walks away from an abusive relationship, who sets boundaries where none previously existed, who decides that her own well-being is more important than meeting societal expectations, these are victories, even if they are not treated as such by mainstream narratives.

Feminism must also redefine victory in ways that account for emotional survival. The expectation that women must always be fighting, always pushing, always proving themselves is itself a form of oppression, a way of ensuring that women remain exhausted and burnt out. There is victory in rest. There is victory in saying no to unreasonable demands. There is victory in refusing to engage with systems designed to deplete energy rather than effect change. A woman who prioritizes her mental health over toxic workplace culture is victorious. A woman who refuses to argue with those who seek only to drain her strength rather than engage in good faith is victorious. A woman who builds spaces of joy, of laughter, of solidarity despite a world that seeks to divide and diminish her, she is victorious.

Victory must also be measured in terms of collective progress, rather than individual achievements alone. The most successful feminist movements have not been those that prioritized singular icons but those that built lasting infrastructures of support, ensuring that the work continues beyond any one person's efforts. This is why mentoring, community-building, and intergenerational activism are essential. The women's liberation movement of the 1960s and 70s did not exist in a vacuum, it was built on the foundations laid by suffragists, labor organizers, and civil rights activists before them. And today's feminism, in turn, must recognize that its victories are not just for the present, but for the future. The most effective way to ensure that gains are not lost is to make sure that new generations are prepared to carry the fight forward, that they are equipped with the knowledge,
128

resources, and confidence to demand more rather than settle for less.

The final lesson in defining victory is recognizing that success does not require permission. Patriarchal systems do not willingly grant power; they must be challenged, pressured, and, in many cases, dismantled. Those who wait for approval, for validation, for confirmation that their actions are worthy will be waiting forever. Victory is not something that is given, it is something that is claimed. And it does not have to look like the victories of the past. It can be quiet. It can be personal. It can be the simple act of refusing to be erased, refusing to be silenced, refusing to accept a world that says women should know their place. Because as long as there are women who refuse, who resist, who push back, the fight is not over, and that, in itself, is a victory worth celebrating.

Victory, when defined by those in power, is always framed in a way that maintains the existing hierarchy. Success is presented as something that must be earned according to rules that were never designed to allow true equity. Women are told that progress means climbing the corporate ladder, securing a seat at the table, proving themselves in male-dominated fields, but too often, these victories require conformity rather than transformation.

The women who make it to the top are often expected to replicate the same oppressive structures that kept others out. They are held up as proof that the system works, as though a handful of exceptional women achieving individual success invalidates the structural inequalities that persist. But feminism has never been about merely placing women into pre-existing systems of power, it is about questioning, challenging, and ultimately reshaping those systems entirely. Victory is not assimilation; it is redefinition. It is not about playing the game better than men; it is about rewriting the rules or refusing to play by them at all.

To reclaim the definition of success, feminism must reject the idea that victory is only measured by conventional forms of power, titles, wealth, status, or visibility. Those are the metrics of capitalism and patriarchy, designed to ensure that only a select few ever reach them while the majority remain locked out. Women have long been told that breaking barriers is enough, that representation alone is the goal, but this is a distraction. A woman CEO who upholds the same exploitative labor practices as her male counterparts is not a feminist victory. A female politician who votes against policies that protect reproductive rights is not a win for gender equality. A woman who gains power at the cost of other women's freedom is not an example of progress; she is proof that the system rewards those who do not threaten its foundations. True victory is not simply about inclusion, it is about transformation, about ensuring that the very structures that govern society are reshaped to serve justice rather than dominance.

This is why it is essential to recognize victories that do not fit traditional definitions of success. A woman who builds a supportive community for other women, ensuring that they have resources, mentorship, and protection in spaces where those things are often denied, she is successful, even if her name is never known outside that circle. A woman who chooses to prioritize caregiving over career, not because she was forced to but because she values that labor and refuses to let capitalism tell her that unpaid work is worthless, her victory is in her autonomy. A woman who walks away from an abusive relationship, from a toxic job, from an environment that demands her silence in exchange for security, she has won because she has chosen herself over the structures that sought to control her.

The refusal to comply with unjust systems is itself a victory. This is why patriarchal forces work so hard to make resistance seem futile. They want women to believe that unless they have completely dismantled oppression, their efforts are

130

meaningless. They want feminists to believe that unless the entire world has changed, their work is a failure. But this is a tactic of control, designed to keep people from realizing that change happens not all at once but in increments, through steady pressure, through persistence. A law protecting reproductive rights may be repealed, but the networks that were built to support women in the face of legal setbacks remain. A workplace may still be discriminatory, but the precedent set by women who refused to accept harassment forces it to change over time. A society may still be shaped by misogyny, but every woman who lives her life on her own terms chips away at the power of those who would prefer she did not.

Feminism must also reclaim the idea of personal victories, not in the sense of individual success within a broken system, but in the way that every woman who resists oppression in her own life contributes to the larger movement. This is particularly important in an era where burnout and exhaustion are real threats to activism. Women are often expected to be constantly engaged in the fight, to sacrifice themselves for the cause, to never take a moment to rest. But a movement that demands endless labor without replenishment is not sustainable. Rest is a revolutionary act. Joy is a form of defiance. A woman who refuses to be consumed by struggle, who finds happiness even in the face of injustice, is engaging in a kind of resistance that is just as crucial as protest or policy change. The goal is not just survival, it is the ability to thrive, to experience pleasure, to create a world where women are not defined by suffering but by the fullness of their humanity.

Victory also means understanding that setbacks do not erase progress. This is one of the hardest lessons for any activist movement to learn because every gain is met with backlash, and every step forward is challenged. It can be demoralizing to watch reproductive rights be stripped away after decades of legal precedent, to see women leaders face relentless attacks simply for existing in spaces men have dominated, to witness new generations being fed the same old lies about their worth. But this does not mean the fight is lost. It means the fight continues. Oppression is not natural, it is enforced. And anything that must be enforced can be dismantled. The forces that seek to strip women of their rights are fighting so hard because they know they are losing. They know that the culture has already shifted in ways they cannot fully control, that even when they pass laws or silence voices, the ideas they fear most have already taken root. And that is a victory.

This is why defining victory on one's own terms is so critical. It allows feminists to see progress where others see defeat. It allows women to recognize their power even when the world tells them they have none. It prevents exhaustion from turning into despair because it reminds us that every act of resistance, no matter how small, contributes to the larger transformation. A single woman refusing to be gaslit into doubting her own experiences, that is a victory. A woman speaking up in a room full of men who would rather she stay silent, that is a victory. A girl learning, for the first time, that she does not have to apologize for taking up space, that is a victory.

And when enough of these victories accumulate, when enough people refuse to accept the world as it is, when enough pressure is applied from enough different angles, the system that once seemed invincible begins to crumble. This is why patriarchy invests so much in convincing women that they are powerless. It knows that the moment they stop believing that lie, the foundations begin to crack.

Victory is not about waiting for permission. It is about claiming power, in whatever form that takes. It is about understanding that the fight is long, but progress is inevitable. And as long as the fight continues, the world will continue to change. And that is the greatest victory of all.

10
Securing the Future

Securing the future is just as critical as achieving victory itself. Too often, movements for justice focus so much on the struggle to win that they fail to plan for what comes next. But history has shown that progress is not permanent. The forces of oppression do not simply disappear when they lose a battle; they regroup, they adapt, they find new ways to regain the power they momentarily lost. Feminists have seen this cycle play out time and time again, every major gain is met with backlash, every inch of ground won must be defended, and every right secured is still vulnerable to being stripped away if the systems that enforce it are not strong enough to withstand attacks.

This is why securing the future must be an active, intentional process. Victory does not sustain itself. It must be reinforced, protected, and institutionalized so that it cannot be easily undone. This means thinking beyond the immediate moment of success and considering how to make that success durable. It means ensuring that when feminist gains are made, whether in legal rights, workplace policies, cultural narratives, or political representation, they are not just temporary shifts, but foundational changes that will remain intact for future generations. The goal is not just to win a fight; it is to reshape the entire playing field so that the same battles do not have to be fought again.

One of the most effective ways to secure the future is by building institutions that outlast any single movement, leader, or moment in time. The greatest feminist victories have not been achieved through isolated efforts but through the establishment of organizations, networks, and infrastructures that ensure continued progress even when individual activists step away. The suffrage movement did not end with the right to vote; it evolved into ongoing political advocacy, ensuring that women were not just legally enfranchised but actively involved in shaping governance. The women's labor movement did not stop at winning fair wages; it built unions and labor protections that would sustain future generations of workers. The fight for reproductive rights has never been about just one court ruling or one piece of legislation, it has required decades of organizing, from underground networks that provided access to birth control when it was illegal, to modern advocacy groups that continue to defend access to abortion and contraception despite constant threats.

Feminism must always be looking ahead, anticipating not just the next fight but the strategies needed to maintain progress over time. This means thinking about how to institutionalize gains in ways that cannot be easily reversed. Laws can be rewritten. Policies can be overturned. But cultural shifts, deeply rooted educational programs, and intergenerational mentorship networks create lasting change. This is why feminist movements must invest in long-term infrastructure, ensuring that victories do not rely solely on the presence of charismatic leaders or momentary bursts of activism. The goal is to make feminist progress so ingrained in the fabric of society that reversing it becomes unthinkable.

A crucial part of this work is mentorship. Every movement needs new leaders, and every victory must be passed down to those who will carry it forward. One of the greatest weaknesses of past feminist movements has been the failure to ensure smooth transitions between generations. Too often, experienced activists burn out, exhausted from years of struggle, without having prepared the next wave of feminists to take over. This leaves progress vulnerable to stagnation or collapse. To prevent this, women who have fought for change must actively mentor younger activists, passing on not just knowledge but strategies, lessons learned, and a clear understanding of the challenges still ahead. This is not just about leadership development, it is about survival. Patriarchy relies on generational amnesia, on each new wave of women believing that their struggles are unique rather than part of a long history of resistance. The more connected feminist movements remain across generations, the harder it becomes for those in power to erase or rewrite the past.

At the same time, securing the future also requires preparing for backlash. No feminist victory has ever gone unchallenged, and the more significant the gain, the more intense the pushback will be. The moment women achieve power in any arena, whether it's political office, corporate leadership, or cultural influence, there is an immediate effort to undermine their success. The pattern is always the same: delegitimization, personal attacks, efforts to roll back progress through legal and political means, and attempts to convince the public that feminist movements have "gone too far." The only way to counter this is to anticipate it, to build safeguards that make it harder for reactionary forces to regain control.

One way to do this is through legal protections. Feminist movements must work not only to secure rights but to embed them in legal frameworks that make them difficult to dismantle. The right to vote, for example, was not just won through activism, it was solidified through constitutional amendments, legal precedents, and ongoing voter advocacy. Workplace protections for women were not just the result of protests; they were reinforced through labor laws, union contracts, and corporate accountability measures. The fight for reproductive justice has never been just about winning access to abortion, it has been about ensuring that those rights are upheld through medical training programs, public health policies, and legal safeguards that make it difficult for conservative politicians to strip them away.

But legal protections alone are not enough. Laws can be overturned. Policies can be rewritten. This is why cultural shifts are just as important as legislative victories. The more deeply feminist values are embedded in everyday life, the harder it becomes to erase them. This means pushing for representation that goes beyond tokenism, ensuring that media, education, and public discourse reflect the realities of women's lives. It means making feminist ideas so commonplace that they are no longer seen as radical but as common sense. This is already happening in some ways, concepts like consent, workplace harassment, and pay equity, which were once controversial, are now widely accepted in many parts of the world. But cultural change is not automatic. It requires constant reinforcement, particularly in times of political regression. Feminists must continue to push these conversations forward, ensuring that every new generation understands not just what has been won, but why it was necessary in the first place.

Another critical aspect of securing the future is recognizing that the fight for gender equality is interconnected with other struggles. Feminism does not exist in isolation; it is deeply tied to issues of economic justice, racial justice, LGBTQ+ rights, environmental sustainability, and global human rights. The more intersectional a movement is, the more resilient it becomes. Opponents of progress rely on the ability to divide and conquer, to pit different marginalized groups against each other, to create the illusion that fighting for one cause means neglecting another. But this is a false choice. The strongest movements are those that understand the connections between different forms of oppression and work together to challenge them. This means building coalitions, forming alliances, and recognizing that securing a feminist future requires dismantling all systems of domination, not just those that explicitly target women.

Ultimately, the only way to secure the future is to make feminism impossible to erase. This means building institutions

that outlast individuals, creating networks that can survive
political shifts, ensuring that feminist history is preserved and
taught, and embedding gender justice into every aspect of
society so that rolling it back becomes unthinkable. It means
preparing for backlash, anticipating attacks, and refusing to be
caught off guard when progress is challenged. It means
mentoring younger generations, passing down knowledge, and
ensuring that the fight does not start from scratch every time a
new challenge arises. It means refusing to accept symbolic
victories in place of real, structural change.

Victory is not the end of the fight. It is the foundation for what
comes next. Those who seek to undo progress are always
working, always planning, always looking for ways to reassert
control. Feminists must be just as relentless, just as strategic,
just as committed to ensuring that every gain is secured,
defended, and expanded. The work is never done, but that is
not a reason for despair. It is a call to action. Because securing
the future is not just about protecting what has been won, it is
about ensuring that future generations inherit a world where
they do not have to fight the same battles all over again.

Securing the future of feminist progress requires more than
just defending victories, it demands foresight, infrastructure,
and an unwavering commitment to resilience. Too often,
movements have celebrated a hard-won gain only to see it
slowly dismantled, eroded by complacency, internal fractures,
and the relentless pushback from those who benefit from
inequality. Progress is not a straight line. It is not a one-time
achievement but a continuous process of building, defending,
and adapting. The forces of patriarchy, capitalism, and
reactionary politics are always watching, waiting for an
opportunity to reclaim lost ground. History has shown that no
right is ever truly secure unless it is actively protected. The
challenge is not just to win, but to ensure that those victories
are not temporary, that they are deeply rooted, integrated into
the very structures of society so thoroughly that reversing them
becomes not just difficult but unthinkable.

One of the most effective ways to secure the future is through institutionalization. Feminist movements have always been strongest when they have built durable structures, organizations, networks, advocacy groups, legal protections, and cultural shifts that extend beyond any single moment of protest or change. The right to vote was not just won and left to stand on its own; it was reinforced by voter education programs, advocacy groups, and legal challenges that ensured women's political participation could not be easily undone. The fight for workplace protections did not end when anti-discrimination laws were passed; it continued through union organizing, workplace monitoring, and continuous legal challenges that held corporations accountable. Feminist movements that fail to institutionalize their victories risk having them reversed as soon as the political winds shift. The key to lasting change is making sure that every gain is cemented within structures that can endure beyond any one leader, movement, or era.

Institutionalization also means ensuring that feminist values are embedded in everyday life, not just in the law. Laws can be rewritten, but cultural shifts are harder to erase. This is why education is one of the most powerful tools for securing the future. The more deeply feminist principles are integrated into school curriculums, workplace policies, media representation, and public discourse, the harder it becomes for reactionary forces to roll back progress. A society where feminist ideas are seen as normal rather than radical is a society where those ideas become self-sustaining, where future generations are raised with an inherent understanding of gender justice rather than having to fight for it anew. This is why feminist movements must invest in storytelling, in media, in literature, in educational initiatives that make gender equality not just a legal expectation but a cultural reality.

Mentorship is another critical component of securing the future. Every generation of feminists must prepare the next, ensuring that knowledge, strategies, and lessons learned are passed down. Too often, movements struggle because they rely too heavily on individual leaders without building a sustainable pipeline of new voices ready to take up the mantle. Patriarchy thrives on the erasure of history, it convinces each new generation that they are alone in their struggle, that their fight is new, that their victories must be won from scratch. But when younger feminists are connected to the wisdom and experience of those who came before them, they are better equipped to recognize patterns, anticipate challenges, and avoid the pitfalls that have weakened past movements. Intergenerational collaboration strengthens feminist resistance, ensuring that the movement does not just react to crises but is constantly evolving, refining its strategies, and staying ahead of those who seek to undermine it.

However, mentorship alone is not enough. Feminist movements must also recognize and address internal divisions that have historically been exploited to weaken progress. One of the most effective ways patriarchy has maintained control is by pitting women against each other, white women against women of color, cis women against trans women, working-class women against professional women, younger feminists against older ones. These divisions are not accidental; they are deliberately cultivated, encouraged by those who benefit from keeping women fragmented and distracted from their common cause. Securing the future means actively resisting these divisions, ensuring that feminism remains inclusive, intersectional, and committed to dismantling all forms of oppression. A movement that only benefits privileged women is not a movement for justice, it is a tool for maintaining the status quo with a different face.

This is why coalition-building is essential. Feminist movements cannot afford to operate in isolation. Gender justice is deeply interconnected with economic justice, racial justice, environmental justice, and labor rights. The more alliances feminist movements build, the more resilient they become. The fight for reproductive rights, for example, cannot be separated from the fight for healthcare access, economic stability, and racial equity. The struggle for workplace equality is inseparable from the fight for labor protections, fair wages, and anti-discrimination policies. When feminist movements align with other justice movements, they build broader coalitions of support, making it harder for reactionary forces to isolate and dismantle them. Solidarity is a form of protection, when different movements support one another, they create a web of resistance that is much harder to break.

Anticipating and preparing for backlash is also a crucial part of securing the future. Feminist movements have faced backlash at every stage of progress, from the suffrage movement to the civil rights era to the modern-day fights for reproductive autonomy and LGBTQ+ rights. The moment a feminist gain is achieved, those who oppose equality begin working to dismantle it. They spread misinformation, manipulate legal systems, use economic pressure, and exploit cultural fears to turn public opinion against progress. Feminists must be prepared for this, not just reacting to backlash as it arises but anticipating it, studying its patterns, and having counterstrategies in place. This means legal defense funds to protect activists from targeted lawsuits. It means media campaigns that proactively counter misinformation. It means building economic support systems for women who face financial retaliation for standing up to discrimination. It means ensuring that every victory is reinforced by mechanisms that make it difficult to reverse.

Another crucial element of securing the future is making feminism politically non-negotiable. The idea that gender justice is a partisan issue is itself a tool of control. Human rights should not be up for debate, yet time and again, gender equality is treated as a political football, subject to the whims of electoral cycles. Feminist movements must work to make gender justice a permanent part of political and legislative frameworks, ensuring that rights are not dependent on who holds power at any given moment. This means electing

140

feminist candidates, holding politicians accountable regardless of party affiliation, and ensuring that policies protecting women and marginalized communities are seen as fundamental, not optional. It also means recognizing that political engagement is not just about voting every few years, it is about sustained pressure, advocacy, and activism that ensures gender justice remains a priority at all levels of government.

Finally, securing the future requires a shift in mindset. Too often, feminists are forced into a defensive position, reacting to crises rather than setting the agenda. While it is necessary to defend against attacks on women's rights, the ultimate goal must be to move beyond playing defense and into shaping the future proactively. This means pushing for ambitious policies that do not just preserve the status quo but actively dismantle systems of oppression. It means demanding more than what has historically been considered possible. It means thinking beyond incremental change and envisioning bold transformations that reshape the foundations of society. Feminism cannot be content with maintaining gains, it must continue expanding them, pushing forward until equality is not just an ideal but a lived reality.

Securing the future is not a passive task. It requires vigilance, strategy, and an unwavering commitment to ensuring that the next generation inherits a world where they do not have to fight the same battles all over again. It means institutionalizing progress, embedding feminist principles into the very fabric of society, and building networks that sustain the fight long after individual activists have moved on. It means recognizing that the work is never finished but that every step forward strengthens the foundation for what comes next. Because the ultimate goal of feminism is not just to win battles, it is to create a world where those battles never have to be fought again. And that future will not secure itself. It must be built, defended, and relentlessly pursued until it is no longer just a vision, but a reality.

Securing the future of feminist progress requires a fundamental shift in how victory is understood. The assumption that progress will naturally sustain itself, that once a right is won, it will remain forever, is a dangerous illusion. The reality is that no right, no gain, no shift in power is ever guaranteed permanence unless it is actively defended. Those who benefit from patriarchy understand this well, which is why they never truly stop fighting, even when they lose a battle. They regroup, they adapt, they study their opposition, and they wait for the right moment to push back, often disguising old forms of oppression under new names. This is why securing feminist victories is not just about holding ground, it is about ensuring that the structures of oppression cannot simply reshape themselves to reclaim lost power. It is about fortifying change so thoroughly that any attempt to reverse it meets not just resistance, but impossibility.

One of the most critical aspects of securing the future is recognizing that oppression does not just operate through overt laws and policies; it is reinforced through culture, economics, and social norms. It is not enough to win legal battles if the underlying narratives that sustain inequality remain unchallenged. If a society continues to devalue women's labor, whether in the workplace or in the home, then wage gaps and economic dependence will persist even if discrimination laws exist. If the media continues to frame women as secondary characters in their own stories, as objects rather than agents, then cultural sexism will continue shaping expectations of what women can and cannot do. If gender roles remain rigidly defined in education, in family structures, in religious institutions, then no amount of surface-level progress will undo the deeper psychological conditioning that keeps women in subordinate positions.

This is why feminist movements must work not just at the level of policy, but at the level of cultural transformation, ensuring that the victories won are not just written into law but embedded into the very fabric of everyday life.

Another essential component of securing the future is economic independence. The reality is that no movement can sustain itself without resources, and no individual can resist oppression without some level of financial security. Patriarchy has long used economic control as a weapon, ensuring that women remain financially dependent and therefore less able to challenge the system. Women who are forced to prioritize survival over activism, who must choose between paying their bills and fighting for their rights, are effectively kept out of the struggle. This is why feminist movements must prioritize economic justice, demanding not only equal pay but workplace protections, paid leave policies, childcare support, and financial safety nets that ensure women are not left vulnerable to economic coercion. It is also why feminist organizations must think strategically about funding, ensuring that they are not reliant on donors or institutions that may seek to dilute their message or control their agenda. Economic self-sufficiency is a form of security, it ensures that movements cannot be easily dismantled by financial pressure, that activists can continue their work without fear of losing everything.

Beyond financial security, feminist movements must also focus on legal resilience. It is not enough to win a court case or pass a piece of legislation if those victories can be undone with the stroke of a pen by the next administration. This is why every legal gain must be fortified with deeper systemic change, ensuring that even if individual laws are challenged, the principles behind them remain embedded in governance. This means integrating feminist perspectives into judicial appointments, into constitutional frameworks, into international human rights agreements that make it harder for reactionary forces to undo progress. It means ensuring that feminist legal scholars are positioned to shape the interpretation of laws over time, recognizing that the law is not static, it is constantly evolving, and those who control its evolution control the future.

Mentorship remains a crucial part of securing feminist victories. The history of feminist movements is filled with moments where knowledge was lost, where hard-earned lessons were not passed down, forcing new generations to repeat the same struggles from scratch. This is not an accident, it is a function of patriarchal erasure, the deliberate rewriting of history to make it seem as though each new generation of women is starting fresh rather than continuing a long legacy of resistance. This erasure weakens movements by severing them from their own power. When younger feminists are unaware of past strategies, of the ways movements before them have been co-opted, infiltrated, or weakened by internal divisions, they become more vulnerable to making the same mistakes. This is why intergenerational dialogue is critical. Those who have fought before must share what they have learned, ensuring that their experiences are not buried but used to strengthen future activism.

However, mentorship must not become a mechanism for gatekeeping. One of the tensions within feminist movements has always been the struggle between preserving wisdom and allowing new voices to lead. Older generations of activists sometimes resist change, believing that their way of fighting is the only way, while younger feminists, frustrated by what they see as outdated tactics, sometimes dismiss the lessons of those who came before. This dynamic is a weakness that patriarchy exploits, turning different factions of feminism against each other instead of allowing them to work together. Securing the future means ensuring that leadership is fluid, that knowledge is shared without imposing rigid hierarchies, that each generation learns from the other rather than competing for dominance.

Another key aspect of protecting feminist progress is preventing the co-optation of feminist language and ideas by institutions that have no real commitment to gender justice. This is a particularly insidious threat because it gives the illusion of progress while maintaining the status quo.

144

Corporations that market themselves as feminist while continuing to exploit female labor, politicians who use feminist rhetoric while voting against women's rights, media outlets that celebrate "empowered women" while reinforcing harmful beauty standards, these are all examples of feminism being used as a brand rather than a movement. This co-optation not only weakens feminism but actively turns it against itself, making it seem as though gender equality has already been achieved while systemic injustices remain intact. Securing the future means remaining vigilant against these forms of manipulation, refusing to allow feminism to be reduced to a slogan while its core goals are sidelined.

Ultimately, securing the future requires an acceptance of the fact that the work will never truly be done. This is not a reason for despair but a recognition of reality. Oppression does not end; it changes shape. Progress is not a destination; it is a continuous process. This means that every victory must be followed by a plan for its preservation, that every gain must be defended as fiercely as it was won, that every generation must prepare the next to continue the fight. Feminism is not a moment, not a single movement, not the work of any one person or group, it is an ongoing struggle, a collective effort to shape a world where justice is not just possible but inevitable.

Securing the future means building movements that are flexible enough to adapt but strong enough to endure. It means refusing to be lulled into complacency, refusing to believe that progress is inevitable, refusing to accept symbolic wins in place of real change. It means understanding that every battle won is just one chapter in a much longer fight, and that the greatest mistake feminism can make is assuming that the work is ever finished. Those who oppose gender justice are always working. They are always planning. They are always preparing for the moment when resistance weakens, when activists become fatigued, when vigilance fades. The only way to counter this is to remain just as relentless, just as strategic, just as committed to ensuring that progress is not only achieved but protected.

And so the final lesson in securing the future is this: feminism cannot afford to be reactive. It must be proactive, shaping the world before its opponents have the chance to do so. It must not just fight against oppression but build the systems that will make oppression impossible. It must not just resist, but create. It must not just demand justice but enforce it. Because the true measure of victory is not just in what is won, but in what is kept, defended, and expanded for generations to come.

11
Leaving a Legacy

Leaving a legacy is not about personal recognition, it is about ensuring that the fight for justice does not have to start from scratch with every new generation. One of the greatest challenges feminist movements have faced over time is the way history is erased, rewritten, or forgotten, forcing each wave of activism to rediscover the lessons that should have already been passed down. Patriarchy thrives on this cycle of amnesia. It relies on the idea that every new generation of women will believe they are alone in their struggle, that they are the first to demand rights, the first to challenge injustice, the first to insist that the world can be different.

This illusion weakens movements, cutting them off from the wisdom, strategies, and hard-won victories of the past. But when knowledge is deliberately preserved and passed on, when movements refuse to let their history be erased, the future becomes stronger. Women no longer have to spend precious time rediscovering old truths, they can build on them, refining and expanding the fight rather than repeating its earliest battles.

This is why mentorship is a fundamental pillar of feminist legacy. Too often, the idea of mentorship is reduced to professional networking or career advancement, but in the context of feminism, it is much broader and deeper. It is about ensuring that knowledge is not lost, that younger activists are equipped with the insights and strategies of those who came before them. It is about passing down not just historical accounts, but the skills needed to sustain movements, how to organize, how to resist co-optation, how to navigate backlash, how to sustain activism over the long haul. Mentorship is the difference between a movement that burns bright for a moment before fading and a movement that endures, continuously adapting and evolving.

For mentorship to be effective, it must be intentional. It is not enough for older generations to simply assume that the next wave will find their way. Feminists who have fought in previous battles must actively reach out, must make themselves available, must understand that part of their role is to ensure that their knowledge does not die with them. Too often, there has been a disconnect between generations, with older feminists feeling dismissed by younger activists, and younger feminists feeling unheard or unrecognized by those who paved the way.

This tension is not an accident, it has been cultivated by those who fear feminist progress. A divided movement is a weaker movement, and nothing weakens feminism more than internal fractures that prevent collective strength. Securing a legacy means bridging these gaps, ensuring that wisdom flows in both directions, that younger generations learn from the past while also bringing new perspectives that challenge and refine the movement's approach.

Beyond mentorship, storytelling is another powerful way to leave a lasting impact. Stories are how people make sense of the world. They are how movements are remembered, how ideas spread, how injustice is exposed, and how resilience is celebrated. Feminist history is full of stories that have been buried, ignored, or distorted, stories of women who led revolutions, who risked everything for change, who challenged systems that seemed immovable and forced them to bend. Recovering these stories, telling them accurately, and ensuring they are not lost again is a critical part of feminist resistance. Every woman who has ever defied expectations, who has challenged power, who has insisted on her right to exist freely, is part of this history. And every woman who ensures that these stories are told, whether through books, conversations, films, classrooms, or activism, is contributing to the preservation of that history.

But storytelling is not just about the past. It is also about shaping the narratives that will define the future. Patriarchy has always relied on controlling the dominant narratives, about gender, about power, about who is capable of leadership and who is not. It tells women they are too emotional to lead, too weak to fight, too divisive to unify, too much of one thing and never enough of another. These narratives are designed to disempower, to keep women questioning themselves rather than challenging the structures that oppress them. One of the most powerful ways to disrupt this is by telling different stories, stories of women who lead, who resist, who build, who refuse to be erased. Stories that show what is possible, that expand the imagination of what feminism can achieve, that inspire the next generation to see themselves not as passive recipients of history but as active participants in shaping it.

Another critical component of leaving a legacy is building networks that can sustain feminist activism beyond any single moment or movement. Too often, feminist organizing has been reactive, mobilizing in response to crises rather than proactively creating structures that ensure lasting change. Networks provide the infrastructure needed to maintain momentum, to ensure that knowledge, resources, and strategies are shared across communities and generations.

These networks can take many forms, grassroots organizations, feminist think tanks, activist coalitions, mentorship programs, digital spaces where ideas are exchanged and amplified. What matters is that they exist, that they are nurtured, and that they are built with longevity in mind. A movement that relies solely on the energy of the present moment will inevitably fade, but a movement that invests in long-term networks will endure.

One of the most dangerous illusions that patriarchy fosters is the idea that feminist victories are permanent, that once a right has been secured, it will remain forever. But history has shown that every gain is vulnerable to being rolled back if it is not actively protected. This is why leaving a legacy means not only celebrating achievements but preparing the next generation to defend them. This requires honest conversations about the cyclical nature of progress, about the ways in which backlash operates, about the strategies that have worked in the past and the ones that have failed. It means recognizing that feminism is not just about achieving new milestones, but about safeguarding the ground that has already been won.

It is also important to ensure that feminist legacies are inclusive. Too often, the history of feminism has been told through a narrow lens, centering the experiences of privileged women while marginalizing the voices of those who have been at the forefront of the most radical and transformative struggles. Leaving a true feminist legacy means amplifying the stories of women of color, working-class women, queer women, disabled women, Indigenous women, those whose struggles have often been ignored or erased but who have been central to the fight for justice. A feminism that only serves the most privileged is not feminism, it is simply another iteration of power replicating itself. The next generation deserves a movement that is expansive, intersectional, and committed to liberation for all.

Ultimately, leaving a legacy is about ensuring that feminism does not become stagnant. The fight for justice is not something that is won and then neatly concluded, it is an ongoing process, one that requires each generation to carry the work forward. The most effective way to do this is to create conditions where new feminists can thrive, where they are not just inheriting a set of principles but are actively shaping the movement in ways that reflect the challenges and possibilities of their time. This means encouraging innovation, embracing change, and understanding that the role of each generation is not just to preserve the past, but to build the future.

Feminism's greatest strength has always been its ability to evolve, to adapt, to push beyond what was once thought possible. The only way to ensure that this continues is by investing in the generations to come, by giving them the tools, the knowledge, and the confidence to take the fight further than it has ever gone before. Because the true measure of a movement's success is not just in what it achieves today, but in how well it prepares those who will carry it forward tomorrow.

Leaving a legacy is not just about passing down stories, but about equipping the next generation with the tools to continue the fight, to challenge power, and to create the world that previous generations only dreamed of. Feminism, like any struggle for justice, is not a static movement. It is alive, evolving with every era, responding to new challenges while remaining grounded in the fundamental principles of equality and liberation. The danger lies in assuming that the work is finished, that because certain battles have been won, the war is over.

The reality is that every generation must recommit to the struggle, must adapt to the conditions of their time, must recognize the threats that may look different from those of the past but operate under the same goal: maintaining systems of oppression, limiting the freedom of those who refuse to submit, and preserving power in the hands of the few.

To truly leave a legacy, feminists must ensure that each new generation understands not only the history of past struggles but also the mechanisms of resistance. Too often, movements focus on what they are fighting against rather than on how to fight effectively. It is not enough to tell young women and gender-oppressed people that they are inheriting a battle, they must be given strategies, networks, and systems of support that make that battle winnable. This is why mentorship, coalition-building, and institutional memory are just as important as political victories. The worst mistake a movement can make is assuming that progress is self-sustaining. Without a plan for continuity, without an infrastructure that outlives any single individual or moment, even the most hard-fought gains can be erased.

One of the most effective ways to ensure that feminism remains a force for change is to cultivate leadership that is both diverse and sustainable. Leadership in feminist movements has historically been shaped by the same structures that feminism seeks to dismantle, hierarchical, centered around singular figures, overly reliant on charismatic personalities rather than collective power. This has led to predictable failures.

When movements place too much emphasis on individual leaders, they become vulnerable; when those leaders step down, are discredited, or pass away, the movement often struggles to continue without them. Feminism cannot afford to be structured like traditional systems of power, it must be decentralized, built on networks rather than figureheads, ensuring that leadership is shared, that movements are not dependent on any one person but are instead fueled by a collective vision.

This is why mentorship should not be about replicating traditional power dynamics, where an older generation simply passes down instructions to the next. It should be a reciprocal relationship, one where younger activists bring fresh perspectives, challenge outdated thinking, and refine the movement's approach while still learning from the experiences of those who came before them. Feminism has suffered from generational divides that have weakened its effectiveness, older feminists accusing younger activists of being too radical, too reckless, or too soft; younger feminists rejecting the work of

those who fought before them as insufficient or outdated.
These tensions, while natural, are also dangerous when they
prevent meaningful collaboration. The strongest movements
are those where generations work together, where knowledge
is shared, and where wisdom is valued without being treated as
unquestionable authority.

Storytelling plays a crucial role in bridging these gaps.
Feminist history is filled with victories that have been erased,
rewritten, or distorted, leaving many young activists unaware
of the struggles that paved the way for the rights they have
today. Patriarchy thrives on this lack of historical continuity,
on making each generation believe they are starting from
nothing, that they have no lineage of resistance to draw from.
This is why storytelling is not just about remembering the past,
it is about ensuring that the present is connected to it, that
younger feminists understand they are part of a larger struggle
that has been fought for centuries. But it is also about ensuring
that these stories do not become stagnant. The past should not
be a template to follow without question, it should be a
foundation upon which new strategies, new perspectives, and
new solutions are built.

Beyond storytelling and mentorship, feminist legacy-building
must also focus on structural change. The feminist movements
of the past have often been criticized for achieving individual
victories without addressing the deeper systems that create
inequality in the first place. It is not enough to have more
women in positions of power if those positions still operate
within patriarchal, capitalist, and white supremacist
frameworks. It is not enough to change laws if the enforcement
of those laws still disproportionately benefits the privileged.
Feminism must go beyond surface-level gains and ensure that
the structures of society are rebuilt in ways that make future
oppression impossible.

This means thinking long-term, investing in institutions that
can carry forward the movement's work beyond any single

moment of progress. It means prioritizing education, ensuring that feminist principles are not just something activists talk about in academic circles but are integrated into schools, workplaces, and communities. It means creating financial and legal support systems that make feminist activism sustainable, that protect those who challenge power from economic and legal retaliation. It means building feminist media, ensuring that the stories told about women and marginalized people are not controlled by the same industries that profit from their oppression.

Feminists must also be aware of how systems of power adapt and respond to progress. One of the great failures of past movements has been underestimating the resilience of oppression. When major victories are won, whether in the form of reproductive rights, workplace protections, or political representation, there is often an assumption that the fight is over. But those who seek to maintain patriarchal control are never idle. They study the movements that threaten their power. They learn from their mistakes. They rebrand their rhetoric, shift their tactics, and find new ways to disguise old forms of oppression. This is why feminist legacy must include vigilance, not just a celebration of past successes but an awareness of how those successes can be undermined.

It is also why intersectionality must remain at the center of feminist work. The most effective way to secure the future of feminism is to ensure that it does not repeat the mistakes of the past, mistakes that have often excluded women of color, working-class women, LGBTQ+ individuals, disabled women, and others who face multiple forms of oppression. A feminism that only serves the most privileged is not feminism at all; it is merely another iteration of power maintaining itself. The next generation must inherit a feminism that is broad in its vision, that does not just fight for small reforms but for a total reimagining of society.

Leaving a legacy is about more than preserving the past, it is about making sure that the future is not constrained by the limitations of previous generations. It is about encouraging younger feminists to think bigger, to demand more, to reject the idea that justice must be won in small, incremental steps. It is about ensuring that the feminist movement remains adaptable, that it does not become so attached to old ways of organizing that it fails to see new opportunities for change. It is about teaching future activists that feminism is not just about fighting against what exists, but about building what comes next.

Legacy is not about looking back, it is about making sure those who come after us have the tools, knowledge, and confidence to move forward. It is about ensuring feminism remains a living, breathing force for justice. The goal is not just to fight for change, but to create a world where each new generation has less to fight for because oppression has been so thoroughly dismantled that it can no longer be rebuilt.

Leaving a legacy means ensuring the next generation does not have to fight the same battles repeatedly. It means breaking the cycle of progress followed by regression, where each new wave of activists is forced to reclaim rights that should have been permanent. Patriarchy thrives on erasing history, convincing younger generations that they are the first to encounter these struggles. This weakens movements, leaving feminists vulnerable to repeating mistakes and overlooking critical lessons.

The best way to disrupt this cycle is by ensuring feminist knowledge, strategies, and victories are not just recorded but actively taught, passed down, and reinforced through culture, institutions, and activism that prioritize longevity over momentary wins.

One of the most dangerous misconceptions about progress is believing that once a right has been won, it will remain intact.

History is filled with examples of rights being stripped away, of movements believing they had reached a turning point only to realize victories were temporary. Voting rights, reproductive freedoms, access to education, none of these have been permanently granted. Each has had to be defended repeatedly as those in power work tirelessly to reclaim control. Feminists cannot assume that a right secured today will still be there tomorrow. Leaving a legacy means preparing for backlash, ensuring that future generations are equipped with knowledge and structures to resist when the next attack inevitably comes.

Feminist legacy must be built on institutions that sustain progress. Individual activists, no matter how brilliant, will eventually step away. Movements that rely too heavily on personalities rather than enduring systems risk collapsing when those individuals are no longer leading the charge. Too often, feminist victories have been linked to a single leader or moment rather than being woven into the structural fabric of society. The right to vote was not truly secured until it was protected by constitutional amendments, reinforced by voting rights acts, and embedded into a system that made it difficult, though not impossible, for reactionary forces to take it away.

The same must be done for every feminist gain. Laws protecting against discrimination must be enforced. Workplace protections must be reinforced through unions and advocacy groups. Reproductive rights must not only be legal but structurally supported through affordable healthcare access, education, and cultural acceptance.

At the same time, feminists must be wary of institutional co-optation. Oppressive systems maintain power by absorbing opposition, rebranding themselves to appear progressive while reinforcing the status quo. Corporations market themselves as feminist while exploiting women's labor, politicians use feminist rhetoric while voting against gender justice, and media celebrates empowerment while enforcing rigid beauty standards. Feminism must remain radical in its demands, not a marketing tool for institutions that have no interest in systemic change. It means recognizing when victories are real and when they are merely symbolic.

Education is one of the most powerful tools in securing a feminist legacy. The more deeply feminist principles are integrated into curriculums, the harder they are to erase. If young people grow up learning about gender justice and the structures of oppression, they are far less likely to be deceived when those in power attempt to rewrite history. But education is not just about schools, it is about media, storytelling, public discourse, and cultural narratives that shape how people understand gender, power, and justice.

Storytelling is crucial. Feminism has always been fueled by the stories of those who resisted, who challenged the world as it was and demanded something better. But too often, these stories have been selectively told, centered on privileged voices while erasing others. A true feminist legacy must ensure that all stories are remembered, the stories of women of color, working-class women, Indigenous activists, queer and trans feminists who have been at the forefront of struggles but have often been ignored. The real power of feminist history lies in the countless, often unnamed individuals whose sacrifices built the movement. Leaving a legacy means preserving these stories so that feminism is understood as a diverse, multifaceted force for change.

Another key aspect of feminist legacy-building is ensuring that activism remains adaptable. The issues feminists face today will not be identical to those in the future, just as the struggles of past generations were shaped by different cultural, economic, and political landscapes. Feminism must be dynamic, shifting and evolving with changing circumstances. This means not resisting new ideas simply because they challenge traditional ways of doing things. It means embracing technological advancements, using digital spaces for activism while also recognizing the dangers of surveillance and online harassment. A movement that is rigid in its thinking will become obsolete. A movement that remains flexible, understanding the need for constant evolution, is one that will endure.

Perhaps the most critical component of leaving a feminist legacy is refusing to settle. Too often, movements have been encouraged to compromise, to accept incremental change rather than demand full justice. While strategic patience and calculated negotiation have their place, there is also a danger in believing that feminism must always wait, that the world is not ready for certain demands, that people must be eased into change rather than confronted with its necessity. This mindset has allowed injustice to persist under the guise of progress. Feminism must not only fight for what seems achievable in the moment, it must push the boundaries of what is considered possible. It must insist on a future where gender justice is not just an aspiration but a reality, where power is not hoarded by the few but shared by all.

Leaving a legacy is about ensuring that feminism does not fade into history as a temporary movement but remains a permanent force for justice. It is about refusing to let the stories of past struggles be erased, refusing to let hard-won victories be taken for granted, refusing to allow the next generation to be convinced that they must start from nothing. The fight is not over, but neither is the progress. And as long as there are those who are willing to resist, to teach, to organize, to demand more, then the legacy of feminism will not only survive, it will grow, thrive, and shape the world for generations to come.

Conclusion
Women's Art of War—NOW

The rules of war have always been written by men, designed to maintain power through brute force, deception, and systemic control. But the battlefield has changed. The tools of oppression have evolved, and so have the strategies of those who resist. Women have never had the luxury of engaging in war on the same terms as men. Our battles have been fought in courts and workplaces, in homes and on the streets, in whispered conversations and loud, public defiance. And now, as technology reshapes every aspect of modern life, it is time to rewrite the rules once again, not to fight on their terms, but to make sure they no longer control the game.

The systems that govern our lives, political, economic, legal, were not built to serve women. They were designed to suppress, exploit, and coerce. They were crafted to maintain power in the hands of the few while ensuring that resistance remains fractured, fatigued, and ineffectual. We have tried reform. We have tried working within the system, believing that if we elected more women, if we won more legal battles, if we proved ourselves "worthy," we could reshape these institutions to work for us. But time and again, those efforts have been met with sabotage, backlash, and the slow erosion of every gain we have made. The lesson is clear: these institutions are beyond saving. The people in power, the politicians, the billionaires, the media moguls, have proven themselves useless at best and complicit at worst. They have failed, and we are under no obligation to keep pretending they deserve to lead.

It is time to cut them loose.

For too long, we have been told that governing ourselves is impossible, that without the existing power structures in place, society would collapse. But technology has already shown us another way. We do not need politicians. We do not need intermediaries who siphon power and wealth while doing nothing for the people they claim to serve. We have the tools to govern ourselves, to educate, vote, and lead without their interference. With modern advancements in AI, blockchain, and decentralized governance, we can eliminate the need for corrupt officials, corporate-backed legislators, and bureaucracies designed to waste time rather than solve problems. The same surveillance systems used to track and control us can be repurposed to hold them accountable, exposing their failures in real-time, making their secrecy and deception impossible. Their power has never been about competence, it has always been about controlling the flow of information, rigging the game so that people remain dependent on them. But with the right tools, we can dismantle their influence entirely.

Imagine a world where voting is instantaneous and uncorruptible, where policy decisions are made directly by the people through decentralized platforms rather than backroom deals. Imagine using AI to analyze government spending in real-time, eliminating waste and ensuring that resources are directed where they are needed. Imagine blockchain-based records that make it impossible for politicians to lie, to manipulate history, to claim credit for work they never did. We already have the technology to create systems that are more transparent, more efficient, and more just than anything our so-called leaders have built. The only thing stopping us is the illusion that we still need them.

The war has always been about control, who has it, who is allowed to wield it, and who is expected to submit to it. Women have been forced to fight for every inch of autonomy, every legal right, every scrap of recognition. But control is shifting. The world is moving too fast for the old systems to keep up, and that presents an opportunity. Every moment of technological advancement weakens their grip, every shift toward decentralization makes their authority more obsolete. Their power relies on our belief in their necessity. Once we stop believing, they become irrelevant.

And when they realize they are losing control, they will fight to keep it. This is why authoritarianism is rising, why reactionary forces are growing more desperate. The backlash we are seeing, against women's rights, against democracy, against free information, is not a sign of their strength. It is a sign of their fear. They know the tide is turning, that their ability to dominate and dictate is slipping away. Their goal is to scare us into submission, to make us believe that without them, there is only chaos. But the truth is, without them, there is only possibility.

The greatest weapon we have is not protest alone, but strategy. We do not need to ask for permission to build something better. We do not need to wait for their approval. We have the means to create a system that works for us, not against us. The tools they have used to suppress us can be turned against them. Surveillance technology, designed to monitor and manipulate, can be used to track corruption, expose injustices, and hold the powerful accountable. Artificial intelligence, trained to serve corporate and governmental interests, can be redirected to ensure fair policy implementation, transparent economic systems, and direct democratic engagement. Social media, used to spread propaganda and misinformation, can be reclaimed to educate, organize, and mobilize.

We are not powerless. We are not at their mercy. We are at a crossroads. We can either keep playing their game, waiting for change that will never come, or we can build the future we actually want. One where power is distributed rather than hoarded, where leadership is earned rather than inherited, where governance is about service rather than control.

This is not a dream. It is a choice.

Women have always adapted to oppression, found ways to navigate unjust systems, outmaneuvered those who sought to keep them powerless. But we no longer need to play defense. The time for adaptation is over. The time for transformation has begun. The tools exist, the knowledge is there, and the will has never been stronger. The question is not whether we can dismantle the old order, it is whether we are ready to seize the moment and do it.

The future is unwritten, but the pen is in our hands. What comes next will not be decided by the men who have spent centuries trying to hold us back. It will not be determined by the politicians who have lied and stalled and compromised us into oblivion. It will be decided by those who refuse to accept their version of reality any longer. The battle is not just about taking power from them, it is about making sure they never get it back.

And when that day comes, when the last remnants of their failed leadership are finally discarded, the world will not mourn their loss. It will wonder why we ever tolerated them in the first place.

The war they started is over. The future belongs to us.

To win a war, one must do more than resist the enemy. One must outthink them, outmaneuver them, and ensure that their weapons of control become their own undoing. The future is not won by those who ask politely for change but by those who take what is needed and refuse to be ruled by outdated institutions that have no place in a world that demands progress. Women have spent centuries working within broken systems, attempting to reshape corrupt power structures in

162

ways that serve justice rather than oppression. That approach has yielded some gains, but it has also proven the limits of reform. The time for asking, for negotiating, for waiting has passed. The only path forward is one where we stop legitimizing the systems that have failed us and start replacing them entirely.

The digital age has created the conditions for this transformation. The structures of the old world, governments bloated with corruption, legal systems designed to protect power rather than distribute it, economic frameworks built on exploitation, are all vulnerable in ways they never have been before. Information, once controlled and hoarded by the few, now moves freely, impossible to contain. Surveillance, designed as a tool of oppression, can be turned against the oppressors. Artificial intelligence, originally programmed to serve capitalist interests, can be repurposed to build economic and social systems that function without middlemen, without billionaires siphoning wealth, without politicians feeding on manufactured division. Blockchain technology, created to facilitate financial transactions, can be adapted to ensure direct democracy, secure elections, eliminate fraud, and remove the need for political representatives who exist only to serve themselves.

The reality is that we do not need the institutions that have governed us. We do not need politicians whose only function is to waste time, enrich themselves, and manufacture crises they have no intention of solving. We do not need corporate-backed lawmakers who spend their careers trading favors and passing laws that preserve their own power. We do not need a legal system that was never built for us in the first place, one that punishes the poor and protects the rich, one that allows violence against women to go unpunished while criminalizing those who fight back. These institutions are obsolete, relics of an era where control was maintained through deception and coercion. But the lie is unraveling. Their authority only holds if we allow it to. Their power only exists because we continue to participate in their broken game.

What happens when we stop?

Imagine a world where voting is not a rigged process controlled by money, gerrymandering, and suppression tactics but an instantaneous, secure transaction performed directly on a decentralized platform. No electoral college, no partisan manipulation, no politicians standing in the way of the will of the people. Imagine a world where economic decisions are made based on collective input rather than the whims of a few billionaires who gamble with global resources for their own profit. Imagine a world where policies are drafted and implemented by direct consensus, where technology removes the need for corrupt intermediaries, where justice is algorithmically enforced with transparency rather than hidden behind bureaucratic red tape. The systems already exist. The only thing stopping us from using them is the outdated belief that we still need rulers.

For centuries, women have been told that power is something given, something granted by those who already hold it. But power is not given. It is taken. And it is time to take it in a way that ensures it can never be stolen again. Women have already proven that they can outthink the system, that they can navigate oppression while building networks of support, resistance, and innovation. What happens when we shift from surviving within the system to dismantling it entirely? When we stop trying to reform institutions that were built to oppress us and start designing systems that make oppression impossible?

The shift has already begun. The collapse of traditional media means that information is no longer dictated by a handful of powerful men deciding what is newsworthy. Social movements no longer require official organizations, funding from donors, or validation from mainstream institutions. They can mobilize

164

in real-time, growing organically, disrupting power structures faster than governments can react. Economic independence is no longer tied to traditional employment, as decentralized finance creates opportunities beyond the wage-slavery model designed to keep people trapped in cycles of dependence. The cracks in the system are everywhere. The next step is widening them until the whole thing falls apart.

One of the greatest lies ever told is that governments exist to serve the people. The truth is that they exist to serve themselves. They exist to maintain the illusion of control, to pacify the masses while ensuring that wealth and power remain concentrated at the top. But what happens when the people take control of their own governance? When they stop voting for politicians who promise change and start voting directly on policies themselves? When they stop waiting for corrupt lawmakers to grant them rights and instead encode those rights into unchangeable digital frameworks that cannot be manipulated or revoked?

This is not a fantasy. It is a necessity. The world is burning, literally and metaphorically. Climate catastrophe is accelerating while those in power refuse to act because their profits depend on continued destruction. The wealth gap has reached levels so obscene that billionaires are making trillions while workers struggle to afford food, rent, and healthcare. Women's rights are being stripped away at a horrifying pace, not because of any moral shift but because control over women's bodies has always been one of the last defenses of a crumbling patriarchy. The men in charge would rather burn the world to the ground than give up their power. So we must take it from them before they succeed.

And we can.

Technology is their greatest weakness because it removes the need for them entirely. It is the weapon they built to control us, but it is the weapon that will undo them. Every oppressive system that has ever existed has relied on controlling information, controlling resources, controlling the ability of people to organize. But they no longer control any of these things. Women do not need permission to build a better world. They do not need a seat at a table that was designed to exclude them. They need to set fire to the table and build something new.

The final lesson of war is this: victory does not come from fighting the enemy on their terms. It comes from making them irrelevant. The politicians, the billionaires, the gatekeepers of power, they have already lost. They just don't know it yet. Every day, their systems grow weaker, more transparent, more unsustainable. The world does not need them. Women do not need them. And soon, they will realize that they no longer have a place in the future we are building.

This is not just a call to action. It is a warning. To those who have built their lives on controlling others, who have used power to hoard wealth, who have relied on our silence and our fear, your time is up. We are not asking for equality anymore. We are not begging for change. We are taking everything you built and repurposing it for something better. You should have listened when we warned you. You should have changed when you had the chance.

But now, it's too late.

The war is over. You lost.

The future belongs to us.

About EATMS Productions

What's happening to women now is not random. It's structural.

Policy, culture, technology, and power are moving in the same direction.

EATMS maps them clearly and shows how to respond.

This title is part of an ongoing body of work. All EATMS Productions titles, across all series, authors, and formats, are components of a single connected project.

Start here: EATMS System Primer — Free Bundle
https://eatms.gumroad.com/l/dyvzbw

For full catalog or inquiries: eatms.me

Free survival booklet + EATMS updates: email "EATMS" to eatms@pm.me

Please feel free to burn part or all of this book, safely, as an effigy.